Families
CARE

Families CARE

Helping Families Cope and Relate Effectively

FACILITATOR'S MANUAL

SUKHI BUBBRA
ANDREA HIMES
COLLEEN KELLY
JOANNE SHENFELD
CHRISTINE SLOSS
LINDA TAIT

camh

Centre for Addiction and Mental Health
Centre de toxicomanie et de santé mentale

Library and Archives Canada Cataloguing in Publication
Families care: helping families cope and relate effectively /
Sukhi Bubbra . . . [et al.].

ISBN: 978-0-88868-705-0 (PRINT)
ISBN: 978-0-88868-706-7 (PDF)
ISBN: 978-0-88868-707-4 (HTML)

1. Substance abuse—Patients—Family relationships. 2. Family psychotherapy.
I. Bubbra, Sukhi II. Centre for Addiction and Mental Health

RC455.4.F3F3515 2008   616.89'156   C2008-900283-0

Printed in Canada

For information on other CAMH publications or to place an order, please contact
Sales and Distribution:
Toll-free: 1 800 661-1111
In Toronto: 416 595-6059
E-mail: publications@camh.net

Website: www.camh.net

This book was produced by the following:
Development: Caroline Hebblethwaite, CAMH
Editorial: Diana Ballon, CAMH; Nick Gamble, CAMH
Design: Mara Korkola, CAMH
Typesetting: Laura Brady
Print production: Christine Harris, CAMH

3368 / 02-2008 / PM081

CONTENTS

MODULE 8
GRIEVING AND COPING

MODULE 9
MANAGING EMOTIONS

MODULE 10
COMMUNICATING EFFECTIVELY WITH A PERSON WHO HAS A SUBSTANCE USE PROBLEM

MODULE 15

SETTING LIMITS WITH A PERSON WHO HAS A SUBSTANCE USE PROBLEM

MODULE 16

HELPING CHILDREN AFFECTED BY SUBSTANCE USE IN THE FAMILY

MODULE 17

FINDING HOPE

MODULE 18

NEXT STEPS

ACKNOWLEDGMENTS

Project team: Sharon Armstrong, Sukhi Bubbra, Andrea Himes, Colleen Kelly, Joanne Shenfeld, Christine Sloss, Linda Tait

Pilot sites and facilitators: Sukhi Bubbra, Andrea Himes, Colleen Kelly, Joanne Shenfeld, Christine Sloss, Linda Tait (CAMH Family Addiction Service); Pam Santon (Addiction Services for York Region)

Feedback and review: Sharon Armstrong, CAMH; Joanna Henderson, CAMH; Baldev Mutta, Punjabi Community Health Centre; Zarsanga Popal, Community Resource Connections of Toronto; Pam Santon, Addiction Services for York Region; Syeda Tahira, Volunteer; Hing Tse, CAMH; Lisa Vettese, CAMH

We also thank the family members who participated in the pilot groups and provided their feedback about the program.

We gratefully acknowledge the generous support of the Stupp/Cohen Families Foundation and its initiative to create the Randy Stupp Fellowship at CAMH.

A NOTE ON LANGUAGE

In many cases, people have substance use and/or mental health problems that have a significant impact on their daily lives, but are not severe enough or do not last long enough to meet the criteria for a diagnosis of any disorder. To reflect the full continuum of harms, in this manual we refer in most contexts to "substance use problems," "problematic substance use" and "mental health problems," and reserve the more categorical terms "substance abuse," "substance dependence" and "mental illness" to describe diagnosable disorders specified by the *Diagnostic and Statistical Manual of Mental Disorders* (DSM-IV). When we discuss the results of research studies, we use the language used by the authors of the study.

Introduction

Who will use this manual?

This manual has been written for therapists working with adults affected by familial substance use. To use this manual, you should be skilled in providing marriage and family therapy and group therapy, particularly from a cognitive-behavioural perspective. You should also have knowledge about the treatment of, and recovery from, substance use problems and concurrent disorders.[1]

Because the program described here is designed as a group treatment, the manual will be most useful to therapists working with groups of family members. Nonetheless, we hope that it can be adapted for use as a structured treatment approach, with either individuals or families, when it is not possible to offer group treatment.

This manual is not a self-help guide. We anticipate that as clients work through this program, they will benefit from the knowledge, teaching, advice, support and encouragement of the facilitators and of other participants.

---

1. In the most formal sense, *concurrent disorders* (or co-occurring disorders) are defined as the presence of at least one diagnosed mental health disorder and at least one diagnosed substance use disorder. Less formally, the term is used to describe co-occurring substance use and mental health problems, whether or not a formal diagnosis has been made.

Why offer programs for family members?

Traditionally, service providers have offered treatment to people with mental health or substance use problems, and have often neglected to involve their family members. We believe strongly in the importance of involving family members in treatment, because:
· family members themselves often need treatment
· family members benefit from treatment
· family members can influence the behaviour of their relatives who have substance use problems, and the outcome of their treatment.

FAMILY MEMBERS NEED TREATMENT

Problematic substance use has an impact far beyond the person who uses substances (Csiernik, 2002). Partners, children, other family members, friends, neighbours, colleagues and associates of a person with a substance use problem all may experience stressful consequences of the person's behaviour. The 2004 Canadian Addiction Survey (Adlaf et al., 2005) revealed that many adult Canadians perceived that in the past 12 months, they had been harmed in some way by others' substance misuse. Of the almost 14,000 respondents to this survey:
· 22 per cent reported having been insulted or humiliated
· 16 per cent had experienced serious arguments or quarrels
· 16 per cent had experienced verbal abuse
· 11 per cent had experienced family or marriage problems
· 11 per cent had been pushed or shoved
· three per cent had been hit or physically assaulted.

In a study conducted in England (Velleman et al., 1993), 50 partners or close relatives of people who misused substances noted ways that they or their families had suffered as a result:
· 94 per cent reported relationship problems such as more arguments, less sex, and less trust and communication
· 88 per cent reported practical problems such as financial difficulties, social isolation and work difficulties
· 82 per cent reported negative emotions such as loneliness, isolation, anxiety, guilt, fear and confusion

· 82 per cent reported mental or physical health problems such as depression, panic attacks, eating disorders, ulcers and raised blood pressure
· 52 per cent reported an increase in their own addictive behaviours such as drinking, smoking, and eating.

Studies in England, Mexico and the United States have found similar negative consequences reported by parents and other relatives of people with substance use problems (Butler & Bauld, 2005; Lewis et al., 2004; Orford et al., 1998).

Nor do the negative consequences disappear—or, necessarily, even decrease—when the person with a substance problem seeks treatment. Despite their wish for the person to recover, family members often experience anxiety and confusion as they deal with the changes and difficulties that occur during the recovery process (Lewis et al., 2004).

It is clear from these data that family members encounter stress from their involvement with the relative with a substance use problem, and that they need help in coping with the negative consequences. Despite this reality, most drug treatment resources in Canada and elsewhere neglect the needs of partners, other family members and friends (Csiernik, 2002; Howells & Orford, 2006). When treatment programs involve family members, they often do so only to help engage the person with a substance use problem in treatment.

FAMILY MEMBERS BENEFIT FROM TREATMENT

In a recent review of studies, researchers concluded that:
· family members who receive family treatment (e.g., family coping skills treatment, behavioural therapy, Al-Anon) have reduced emotional distress
· those who receive coping skills treatment experience improved coping
· partners who receive behavioural couples therapy experience happier relationships, fewer separations, a lower risk of divorce and less domestic violence than those whose substance using partners receive no family treatment (O'Farrell & Fals-Stewart, 2003).

In a recent study, researchers in England found that spouses who received individual counselling aimed at improving coping, safety, relational skills, problem solving and emotion management showed significant decreases in psychological symptoms over the course of treatment, and that these changes were maintained for 12 months after treatment (Howells & Orford, 2006).

Another study demonstrated that children affected by familial substance use can benefit from their parents receiving treatment—as evidenced by improved functioning—even when they themselves receive no treatment (Kelley & Fals-Stewart, 2002).

FAMILY MEMBERS INFLUENCE THE PERSON WITH A SUBSTANCE USE PROBLEM

Research has demonstrated that family involvement in treatment both increases the rate of treatment initiation and improves treatment outcomes for the person who uses substances (Stanton, 2004).

Family treatment can help to increase the likelihood of a person with a substance use problem entering treatment, for example by helping to change family patterns or problems that are impeding the person's motivation to enter treatment (Hser et al., 1998). One successful model is Community Reinforcement and Family Training (CRAFT; Miller et al., 1999).

Family treatment can also help those who are already in treatment. Rowe & Liddle (2003) found that these people demonstrate less substance use, better medication compliance and better family and relational functioning than those whose families are not involved in treatment. One form of family treatment, behavioural couples therapy, has been studied extensively and has proved effective in reducing substance use and improving relationships (O'Farrell & Fals-Stewart, 2003). Another study showed that when family members attended Al-Anon, their relative with a substance use problem was significantly more likely to continue attending Alcoholics Anonymous (McBride, 1991).

No matter how they behave or what choices they make, partners, other family members and friends do influence the person who has a substance use problem, and receiving treatment themselves can help increase the positive impact of their influence. Family members can provide consequences for the person's behaviour, exert appropriate pressure, encourage and support the person, and provide information. For example, they can:

· learn how to avoid reinforcing problematic substance use (e.g., avoiding telling the person that he or she is more fun after a few drinks) and how to set limits around this behaviour

· learn how to avoid enabling the person's substance use (e.g., avoiding calling the person's employer with a story that covers up the fact that he or she can't make it to work because of substance use) and how to allow the person to experience the full consequences of his or her use

· learn about the recovery process and how to reinforce the person as he or she takes steps toward recovery

· improve their skills in problem solving, regulating their emotions, resolving conflicts and communicating, all of which can improve their relationship with the person who has a substance use problem.

The Families CARE program

WHAT IS FAMILIES CARE?

Families CARE is a program that aims to help family members Cope And Relate Effectively with the person who has a substance use problem, not only to support the person's recovery but also to enhance their own well-being. The program offers education, support and skills development. Though eclectic, Families CARE is rooted in a cognitive-behavioural approach. Family members learn about, discuss and practise such skills as coping, grieving, dealing with emotions, solving problems, setting goals, communicating, setting limits, supporting and responding to the person with a substance use problem, and helping children affected by a family member's substance use.

Families CARE is not an "intervention." There has been a great deal of publicity about intervention approaches, particularly the Johnson Institute Intervention, and many family members ask about this method. We do not use or recommend this approach for several reasons:

· The research data do not support the intervention method, which engages only 20 per cent of potential clients in treatment, a significantly lower percentage than other approaches (Stanton, 2004). This low rate of success seems to derive from the fact that most family members who begin the process are not able to follow through on the intervention.

· Research suggests that clients who do engage in treatment following an intervention are at higher risk of relapsing than are clients who engage in treatment through less confrontational methods (Loneck et al., 1996).

· The intervention approach focuses on getting the person with a substance use problem into treatment, and may do nothing to help family members reduce their distress or cope better with their situation. (In fact, if the intervention is aborted prior to completion or if it fails, family members may actually become more emotionally distressed.) In addition, a treatment designed only to get a person into treatment does not help family members support the person and deal with issues arising from the person's treatment and recovery.

· While the goal of the intervention approach is only to help a person begin treatment, Families CARE helps family members of people who may be at various stages of treatment and recovery, not just pre-treatment. (This is also true of other documented and researched treatment methods for family members, such as CRAFT and behavioural couples therapy, which—though otherwise successful models—are not relevant to groups of family members who may have differing needs with regard to the person in their respective families who has a substance use problem.)

WHO CAN BENEFIT FROM FAMILIES CARE?

Families CARE is intended for adult family members—including partners, adult children, parents, siblings, or even friends or ex-partners of people who are engaging or have engaged in problematic substance use, and who may or may not be in treatment. For the sake of simplicity, we will refer to these concerned others as "family members" or, in the context of the treatment sessions, as "group members" or "participants."

Relationship of family members to the person with a substance use problem

Family members may vary in their level of current involvement with the person who uses substances, ranging from living with the person to having little contact with him or her. Given this, the Families CARE program may be offered by a substance use treatment agency to families of its clients (though the person with a substance use problem does not participate in the group), or may be offered as a service for family members even when the person with a problem is not a client of the agency.

Mental health of family members

Many family members may be struggling with mental health issues, often in part because of the stress of their relationship with the person who has a substance use problem. Prior to beginning the program, family members should be screened to determine their mental health status. If they have serious mental health problems (e.g., severe depression or anxiety, bipolar disorder, a personality disorder or an eating disorder), have substance use problems, or are at risk of violence or suicide, they will need additional services and should be given appropriate referrals before beginning the program. They may need to increase their level of stability in order to participate successfully in the group treatment. Family members who have mental health problems may also be helped by treatment from an individual therapist while completing the Families CARE program.

Involvement of the person with a substance use problem

The Families CARE program is intended only for family members, and not for the person in the family who has a substance use problem. This is because the treatment of family members should not depend on:

· the willingness or ability of the person who uses substances to participate in treatment (some people with substance use problems may not co-operate or may not be ready to engage in treatment; others may not be able to attend treatment because they live far away, are in jail or a residential treatment facility or hospital, or have schedule conflicts)

· the amount of contact the family members currently have with the person who has a substance use problem (family members who have ended their relationship with a person who uses substances may still need and benefit from treatment)

· where a person who uses substances is in his or her substance use or recovery (family members may benefit from treatment when a family member is just beginning to exhibit symptoms of substance use problems, is experiencing severe problems, is beginning treatment, is in early or later recovery, or has relapsed).

As mentioned earlier, family members themselves typically struggle to cope and may be experiencing mental health difficulties. Consequently, their treatment is important: it may help to reduce their preoccupation with the difficulties, needs and goals of the person who has a substance use problem, and may enable them to identify their own difficulties, needs and goals. Further, as we have noted, their treatment—with or without the involvement of the person who uses substances—may lead to positive changes for that person (Miller et al., 1999; Stanton, 2004).

Family therapy including the person with a substance use problem can be helpful, but should be done outside of this program.

When running the program, you may discover that the family members themselves vary in their use of substances, from no use ever, to past use, to current problematic use. Some family members use substances themselves to cope with their relationship to a person who has a substance use problem. Although the program can help family members learn healthier methods of coping, family members who have significant substance use problems should be excluded from the program and be directed instead to substance use treatment.

The development of Families CARE

BACKGROUND

In 1997, the Centre for Addiction and Mental Health (CAMH) opened the Family Addiction Service (FAS) to meet the needs of family members of people with substance use problems. Since then, FAS therapists have worked with family members both individually and in groups.

Initially the group program was primarily supportive, but over time it began to address particular topics, such as self-care, boundaries and hope. Various groups were run at different sites, by different therapists, with different topics and in different ways. Following most educational evenings or series of groups, staff elicited written feedback from the clients.

In March 2006, the FAS hired a psychologist to help review, refine, consolidate and manualize the group programs being offered. This psychologist:
· observed some of the educational evenings and groups, as well as similar groups offered in other programs
· read the feedback forms from family members, which provided information on what they believed was helpful about their treatment and what they wished could have been different
· solicited feedback from the therapists who facilitated the groups and educational evenings (through surveys, interviews and group discussions) and from FAS board members
· reviewed research articles and books on treatment relevant to the support offered in the FAS, looking specifically for empirically validated approaches that could be adapted to the needs of the FAS's clients.

PRIORITIES

For a year after this initial process, the FAS team expanded the program, incorporating material from a variety of sources. This program development was based on the following priorities:
· using empirically validated treatment
· meeting the needs of our diverse clientele
· providing support
· facilitating skills development
· providing education.

Each of these areas is discussed below.

Using empirically validated treatment

Two of the treatments best validated by empirical data are Community Reinforcement and Family Treatment (CRAFT; Stanton, 2004), a cognitive-behavioural treatment program designed to help partners or other family members to enter treatment; and behavioural couples therapy (O'Farrell & Fals-Stewart, 2003), a behavioural treatment program for both partners.

Like these two programs, we chose to use a cognitive-behavioural approach with our family members.

Meeting the needs of our diverse clientele

We had to develop a program that could be useful for various types of family members (e.g., partners, adult children, parents, siblings, close friends, ex-spouses), with varying levels of involvement and contact (ranging from living with the person who has a substance use problem to having no current contact), and whose family member may be at varying points in the recovery process (ranging from denial of a substance use problem to maintenance of recovery). The program also had to be flexible enough to be used for family members of different ethnocultural and religious backgrounds and in different settings.

Providing support

Research has long shown that support plays an important role in helping people cope with difficult circumstances. Unfortunately, due to the stigma of substance use and mental health problems, some family members become isolated and do not receive support from others. Treatment offers family members the opportunity to experience professional support and so to reduce their isolation and shame.

Research has demonstrated that family members who take part in group programs such as Al-Anon experience decreased emotional distress and personal problems, due perhaps in part to the support they receive (O'Farrell & Fals-Stewart, 2003). These findings are supported by the feedback from the FAS's clients, which demonstrated an appreciation of the group's providing validation and support. The clients also appreciated the fact that they were accountable to the group for the changes that they had agreed to make. We decided to offer our program primarily through a group format not only because it is cost- and resource-effective, but also because it is an effective intervention. A recent review of treatment studies demonstrated that there was no difference in outcomes between group therapy for family members and family therapy (Stanton & Shadish, 1997).

Facilitating skills development

As well as demonstrating the benefit to family members of education and support, research has also shown benefits from skills training through family, couples or family group therapy, including greater decreases in emotional distress, increases in coping skills, and greater positive changes in the behaviour of the person with a substance use problem (O'Farrell & Fals-Stewart, 2003; Rychtarik & McGillicuddy, 2005; Smith & Meyers, 2004; Stanton & Shadish, 1997). Treatment programs that help family members learn new ways of behaving seem to be the most successful in helping both the family member and the person with a substance use problem.

Al-Anon has long emphasized the importance of family members identifying their powerlessness over those who engage in problematic substance use, and accepting that they cannot change another person. However, research has demonstrated that family members do influence one another and can support the recovery of another person (Meyers & Wolfe, 2004). CRAFT has been designated the most effective program for concerned others of adults who have problems with alcohol or other drugs and who are not in treatment (Stanton, 2004). CRAFT is a highly structured cognitive-behavioural treatment approach that helps concerned family members learn new skills in dealing with the person with a substance use problem, with the result of improving their own functioning and that of the person who uses substances (e.g., at least 64 per cent of those identified in the study as "drinkers or drug users" entered treatment) (Miller et al., 1999). Behavioural couples therapy is another intervention that helps clients make behavioural changes in how they respond to each other. It too has demonstrated improvements in the functioning of both spouses (O'Farrell & Fals-Stewart, 2003).

We built on this evidence by incorporating a skills development component into our model.

Providing education

In response to frequent requests from family members for information on a variety of topics, we incorporated an educational component into our model. We believe that when family members are provided education, they are more knowledgeable about their relative's situation, about substance use and concurrent disorders, and about treatment options; more realistic in their expectations; more firm in setting limits with the person who has a substance use problem; more supportive of the person's positive gains; and more able to make informed decisions about their own behaviour and responses. A recent study in Sweden demonstrated that spouses of alcoholics exhibited improved coping and decreased distress after receiving one individual information session in which they were educated on coping strategies, alcohol dependence and its effects on the alcoholic partner and the family, and on addiction treatment and social services (Zetterlind et al., 2001).

PILOT STAGE

Stage 1

After the first draft was completed, the revised program—now called Families CARE—was offered by six therapists at two of CAMH's facilities. The program comprised three elements.

The first component was a two-hour educational evening for family members that covered substance use and concurrent disorders and their effects on families; the stages of change; the process of recovery and its effect on families; and treatment options for families and for people using substances. Most of the material for this seminar came from modules 2 and 14 of this manual. This educational evening was presented twice, each time by at least two therapists, to 69 family members (24 at one session and 35 at the other). Participants were told at this educational evening that if interested and if they had not already done so, they could contact a therapist and schedule a screening and assessment interview for further services (including individual, couple or group therapy within the Family Addiction Service).

The second component of the program was the screening and assessment interview to determine family members' eligibility for and interest in participating in the group program.

The third component consisted of eight weeks of group treatment, whose topics were determined by the interest of group members and which are contained within this manual. The group was offered three times, and each was facilitated by two therapists. A total of 31 people participated (25 women and six men), whose relationship to the person with a substance use problem varied.

Stage 2

After the second draft of the program was completed, Families CARE was again offered at CAMH, by seven therapists at two sites over a period of 18 months. This time, 457 people took part in 11 large educational sessions (an average attendance of 42). Of these people, 148 (114 women and 34 men) subsequently took part in a Families CARE group, and 124 completed the program. While each group began with an average of 10 members, the average number of participants per session was seven.

Families CARE was also offered outside of CAMH, in conjunction with Addiction Services for York Region, in order to determine whether our materials could be used successfully in another setting and by someone who was not part of our team, and with a different group of family members. The participants and facilitator of this pilot provided feedback to help us refine the materials.

FEEDBACK

At various points in the development of Families CARE, many professionals and clients provided feedback on the program.

During the first stage of the development process, we asked every family member who attended an educational evening or small group session to fill in our feedback form. We used the information received to help us revise the respective sessions. During the second stage, we asked for feedback from family members who attended an educational evening and then, if they went on to participate in a group, upon completion of the program. Unfortunately we did not obtain written feedback from participants who did not complete the group program.

Educational evening

Family members who attended the educational evenings rated their satisfaction level with the content and presentation on a seven-point scale, with 1 being "not at all satisfied" and 7 being "very satisfied." The average rating for content was 5.8, and for presentation 5.7. Most participants responded positively about the content, indicating that they found it informative, comprehensive, relevant and practical. Almost as many people mentioned particular topics that they found helpful, such as the stages of change. Other respondents said they found the presenters knowledgeable, caring, understanding and responsive, and skilled in creating an open, relaxed, positive and comfortable atmosphere. A large number expressed their appreciation for the interaction and the social support they experienced during the discussions and the question and answer periods. The participants said they most liked the educational evening because they felt validated, affirmed, supported and encouraged.

When asked what they liked least about the educational evening, family members indicated that it was too short and did not cover enough information, or that the information was not specific to their situation. Many wanted to know more about concurrent disorders, types of drugs and their effects, harm reduction, substance use treatment, recovery and maintenance. Many people also wanted to spend more time learning how they could respond and relate to the person in their lives with a substance use problem. (For those who went on to attend the group sessions, these issues were dealt with in much greater detail in that context.) Some participants said that the group was too big (attendance was as high as 60) and involved too much interaction (this was sometimes defined as other participants asking inappropriate or personal and over-specific questions). Others felt that the format did not allow enough time for questions.

After the educational evening, family members shared their reactions to the evening. The most common responses were that family members had:
· learned new ways of responding to the person with a substance use problem
· developed a greater understanding of addiction, treatment, recovery (including realistic expectations), relapse prevention and the experiences of families and of people with substance use problems
· learned about resources for themselves and for the person with a substance use problem
· started to focus more on their own needs; and to feel less alone and more supported, reassured, and more hopeful.

Group sessions

Group members rated the teaching and discussion component and the homework exercises on a five-point scale, with 1 being "not at all helpful" and 5 being "very helpful." The average rating for the teaching and discussion was 4.8, and for the homework 4.3. Most participants liked the social aspect of the group, including the social support and their interaction with other group members. Others mentioned the warm and safe environment created, and the skilled facilitation of the leaders. Many expressed appreciation for the content and the educational component, noting how much they had learned and grown, and how much they had appreciated the topics, handouts and homework exercises.

When asked to identify what they had not liked about the program, participants' comments generally centred on their opinion that the sessions were too short and too few, and that the program did not include a "reunion" session.

How to use the Families CARE manual

The Families CARE program comprises 18 modules, including sample introductory and closing sessions. Different treatment settings and different populations have distinct resources, needs and structures, so the manual and materials are designed to be tailored your program—you do not need to offer all 18 modules.

For example, some facilities or programs may offer full day or weekend workshops, others might offer a time-limited series of individual or group sessions, and yet others might offer ongoing long-term groups.

In describing the program, we will assume that you are offering time-limited outpatient group sessions, which is probably the most common and beneficial way in which family treatment is offered. Weekly sessions offer family members ongoing support and guidance for an extended period, without saturating them with too much information at once, while providing opportunities to practise what they are learning at home between sessions.

CHOOSING MODULES

We recommend that the group program run for at least 10 sessions, to enable the participants to develop supportive relationships and to change the ways they cope and deal with their situation. At CAMH, as noted earlier, we start with a two-hour educational evening (the equivalent of two sessions), open to all, in which we present information on substance use problems and recovery, and their effects on families. This is followed by eight closed group sessions for attendees of the educational evening who would like additional support and education. We then offer optional workshops on specific topics that may not be relevant to all the group members.

There is enough material in the manual for at least 18 sessions. However, many modules could be extended over multiple sessions, so if you are able to offer a longer-term or ongoing group you will have plenty of material to do so. Feedback from the pilot stage suggests that some family members appreciate receiving treatment beyond 10 weeks so, if you offer a time-limited group, you may choose to provide one or more booster or reunion sessions at a later date. It is becoming increasingly evident that booster sessions can help clients sustain gains in the longer term (Connors & Walitzer, 2001; Eyberg et al., 1998).

If you provide only short-term treatment it will not be possible to cover all 18 modules, so the facilitators will need to determine which modules are the most relevant (a pre-treatment survey, through which you can obtain clients' input on the topics they would like to be addressed, is included as Appendix 1 of this introduction). We recommend that you devote at least one session to each module (excluding the final session), because covering more than one module in a single session would be difficult and may overwhelm participants. However, as noted above, you may wish to dedicate more than one session to a particular topic if it is particularly salient or problematic for the participants.

There is no set order in which to provide the sessions. However, we recommend that, after introducing the program in Module 1: Starting Out, you present Module 2: Understanding Substance Use Problems and Their Effect on Families, which is the most informational session and the least demanding for group members. We cover this session in our educational evening.

We suggest that you then choose at least two modules that are designed to improve family members' well-being and to prepare them for later topics that may be more emotionally demanding. These modules are:
· Module 3: Taking Care of Yourself
· Module 4: Finding Support
· Module 5: Managing Stress
· Module 6: Using Religious and Spiritual Resources.

We strongly advise you to then deal with crisis management and safety (Module 7: Staying Safe and Managing Crises). Participants must be able to maintain their safety if they are going to deal with their emotions, make changes in their relationships and be successful in treatment.

You can then move on to one or both of two modules that involve deeper emotional processing and the learning of emotion management skills:
· Module 8: Grieving and Coping
· Module 9: Managing Emotions.

We suggest that only after providing information, helping to bolster family members' well-being, ensuring safety, and dealing with emotions do you begin tackling the change-oriented modules and those specifically related to the person with a substance use problem. We recommend that you begin with one of the modules that cover communication, because these modules offer family members tools to help them make changes in their relationship with the person who has a substance use problem. The relevant modules are:
· Module 10: Communicating Effectively with a Person Who Has a Substance Use Problem
· Module 11: Problem Solving
· Module 12: Setting Goals and Making Change Happen
· Module 13: Responding to a Person Who Has a Substance Use Problem
· Module 14: Supporting the Recovery of a Person with a Substance Use Problem
· Module 15: Setting Limits with a Person Who Has a Substance Use Problem.

Module 16: Helping Children Affected by Substance Use in the Family may go anywhere in the cycle or can be offered as a standalone workshop. At CAMH, we have provided it as a workshop that family members who have attended our groups can attend if it is relevant to them.

Finally, we recommend that if you have a time-limited group, you end with Module 17: Finding Hope, and Module 18: Next Steps. Even if your program is ongoing, you may wish to periodically incorporate some of the components of

Module 18 to help family members evaluate what they have done and to determine next steps.

This information is summarized in the table below.

Order of modules*

A. PROVIDING BASIC INFORMATION

Module 1: Starting Out

Module 2: Understanding Substance Use Problems and Their Effect on Families

B. IMPROVING FAMILY MEMBERS' WELL-BEING

Module 3: Taking Care of Yourself

Module 4: Finding Support

Module 5: Managing Stress

Module 6: Using Religious and Spiritual Resources

C. ENSURING SAFETY

Module 7: Staying Safe and Managing Crises

D. DEALING WITH EMOTIONS

Module 8: Grieving and Coping

Module 9: Managing Emotions

E. COMMUNICATING AND MAKING CHANGE

Module 10: Communicating Effectively with a Person Who Has a Substance Use Problem

Module 11: Problem Solving

Module 12: Setting Goals and Making Change Happen

Module 13: Responding to a Person Who Has a Substance Use Problem

Module 14: Supporting the Recovery of a Person with a Substance Use Problem

Module 15: Setting Limits with a Person Who Has a Substance Use Problem

Module 16: Helping Children Affected by Substance Use in the Family†

F. ENDING

Module 17: Finding Hope

Module 18: Next Steps

---

* It is recommended that at least one module from each lettered section be completed before moving on to those in the next section. Within most sections, the modules may be completed in any order. Certain modules may be omitted, depending on time available (see page 15 for details).

† May be offered anywhere in the cycle, or as an optional standalone workshop.

COMPONENTS OF THE MANUAL

For each module, we provide objectives and a session outline, teaching points and a discussion of key topics, and handouts.

Objectives and session outline

The module objectives help facilitators to quickly see what each module covers. They will also help you to stay focused during the sessions on what you hope clients will learn. The session outline provides an at-a-glance guide to the format of each module.

Teaching points and discussion

This part of each module will help you prepare for the session and guide you in conducting the sessions. The material was developed by therapists who have facilitated the program and contributed to this project. It includes suggestions for how to cover topics, such as:

· ways to explain or define concepts
· questions to ask to promote discussion
· exercises to help clients reflect on a topic.

These session protocols also provide advice and background information to help you handle topics knowledgeably and effectively. Ideally you will have the opportunity to become comfortable with this material prior to each session, and will need to refer to it only occasionally during sessions.

Handouts

Each module includes handouts that provide information, clinical exercises and home practice for clients to use during the sessions and at home. The teaching points sections provide instructions for when and how to use the handouts. The home practice assignments are important, so you should emphasize the need for family members to complete the assignments.

We have found it helpful to give the group members binders in which to keep their handouts. Once you have decided what modules you will cover, you can fill the binders with all the material you will use. Alternatively, you can distribute hole-punched handouts each week. If you fill the binders at the beginning of the group, it avoids the need to distribute handouts during each session, which can be distracting, and it enables participants who miss a session to look over the material at home and do the home practice.

NOTE: This manual is intended only as a guide, and should not supersede the perceptions and judgment of the facilitators. We expect that you will adapt the procedures, exercises, information and handouts to make them relevant and helpful to the family members you work with.

References

Adlaf, E.M., Begin, P. & Sawa, E. (2005). *Canadian Addiction Survey (CAS): A National Survey of Canadians' Use of Alcohol and Other Drugs: Prevalence of Use and Other Harms: Detailed Report.* Ottawa: Canadian Centre on Substance Abuse.

Butler, R. & Bauld, L. (2005). The parents' experience: Coping with drug use in the family. *Drugs: Education, Prevention, and Policy, 12* (1), 35–45.

Connors, G.J. & Walitzer, K.S. (2001). Reducing alcohol consumption among heavily drinking women: Evaluating the contributions of life-skills training and booster sessions. *Journal of Consulting and Clinical Psychology, 69* (3), 447–456.

Csiernik, R. (2002). Counselling for the family: The neglected aspect of addiction treatment in Canada. *Journal of Social Work Practice in the Addictions, 2* (1), 79–92.

Eyberg, S.M., Edwards, D., Boggs, S.R. & Foote, R. (1998). Maintaining the treatment effects of parent training: The role of booster sessions and other maintenance strategies. *Clinical Psychology: Science and Practice, 5* (4), 544–554.

Howells, E. & Orford, J. (2006). Coping with a problem drinker: A therapeutic intervention for the partners of problem drinkers, in their own right. *Journal of Substance Abuse, 11* (1), 53–71.

Hser, Y., Maglione, M., Polinsky, M.L. & Anglin, M.D. (1998). Predicting drug treatment entry among treatment-seeking individuals. *Journal of Substance Abuse Treatment, 15*, 213–220.

Kelley, M.L. & Fals-Stewart, W. (2002). Couples- versus individual-based therapy for alcohol and drug abuse: Effects on children's psychosocial functioning. *Journal of Consulting and Clinical Psychology, 70* (2), 417–427.

Lewis, V., Allen-Byrd, L. & Rouhbakhsh, P. (2004). Understanding successful family recovery in treating alcoholism. *Journal of Systemic Therapies, 23* (4), 39–51.

Loneck, B., Garrett, J.A. & Banks, S.M. (1996). The Johnson Intervention with four other methods of referral to outpatient treatment. *American Journal of Drug and Alcohol Abuse, 22,* 363–375.

McBride, J.L. (1991). Assessing the Al-Anon component of Alcoholics Anonymous. *Alcoholism Treatment Quarterly, 8* (4), 57–65.

Meyers, R.J. & Wolfe, B.L. (2004). *Get Your Loved One Sober: Alternatives to Nagging, Pleading, and Threatening.* Center City, MN: Hazelden.

Miller, W.R., Meyers, R.J. & Tonigan, J.S. (1999). Engaging the unmotivated in treatment for alcohol problems: A comparison of three intervention strategies. *Journal of Consulting and Clinical Psychology, 67,* 688–697.

O'Farrell, T.J. & Fals-Stewart, W. (2003). Alcohol abuse. *Journal of Marital and Family Therapy, 29* (1), 121–146.

Orford, J., Natera, G., Davies, J., Nava, A., Mora, J., Rigby, K. et al. (1998). Tolerate, engage or withdraw: A study of the structure of families coping with alcohol and drug problems in South West England and Mexico City. *Addiction, 93* (12), 1799–1813.

Rowe, C.L. & Liddle, H.A. (2003). Substance abuse. *Journal of Marital and Family Therapy, 29* (1), 97–120.

Rychtarik, R.G. & McGillicuddy, N.B. (2005). Coping skills training and 12-step facilitation for women whose partner has alcoholism: Effects on depression, the partner's drinking, and partner physical violence. *Journal of Consulting and Clinical Psychology, 73* (2), 249–261.

Smith, J.E. & Meyers, R.J. (2004). *Motivating Substance Abusers to Enter Treatment: Working with Family Members.* New York: Guilford Press.

Stanton, M.D. (2004). Getting reluctant substance abusers to engage in treatment/self-help: A review of outcomes and clinical options. *Journal of Marital and Family Therapy, 30* (2), 165–182.

Stanton, M.D. & Shadish, W.R. (1997). Outcome, attrition, and family-couples treatment for drug abuse: A meta-analysis and review of the controlled, comparative studies. *Psychological Bulletin, 122* (2), 170–191.

Velleman, R., Bennett, G., Miller, T., Orford, J., Rigby, K. & Tod, A. (1993). The families of problem drug users: A study of 50 close relatives. *Addiction, 88,* 1281–1289.

Zetterlind, U., Hansson, H., Åberg-Örbeck, K. & Berglund, M. (2001). Effects of coping skills training, group support, and information for spouses of alcoholics: A controlled randomized study. *Nordic Journal of Psychiatry,* 55 (4), 257–262.

Pre-treatment survey

We would like to get an idea about your needs and hopes with regard to participating in Families CARE. To help us design the most useful program for you, please take a moment to answer the following questions.

What counselling or therapy you have received in the past to help you deal with a family member who has a substance use problem?

☐ individual counselling or therapy
☐ family counselling or therapy
☐ couple counselling or therapy
☐ group counselling or therapy
☐ information session
☐ support group
☐ other: _____

What would you like to get out of participating in Families CARE?

_____

_____

_____

What skills or knowledge would you like to gain during Families CARE?

_____

_____

_____

From the list below, please check any topics that you would like to cover in the program:

☐ understanding substance use problems and their effects on partners and other family members
☐ managing stress (from multiple sources)
☐ taking care of yourself
☐ getting social support and dealing with stigma
☐ finding and using religious and spiritual resources
☐ finding hope
☐ staying safe and managing crises
☐ grieving and coping with losses
☐ managing sadness and depression
☐ managing anxiety and worry

☐ managing shame and guilt
☐ managing anger
☐ communicating effectively with a person who has a substance use problem
☐ responding to a family member with a substance use problem
☐ supporting the recovery of a family member with a substance use problem
☐ maintaining boundaries and setting limits
☐ solving problems
☐ setting goals and making changes
☐ helping children affected by substance use in the family
☐ other:_____

_____

Sample opening or closing exercises

MINDFULNESS EXERCISES

Mindfulness exercises help people to focus on the "here and now," and become more aware of themselves, their behaviour and their environment. There are many good resources on mindfulness, such as these books and CDs by Jon Kabat-Zinn:

Full Catastrophe Living: Using the Wisdom of Your Body and Mind to Face Stress, Pain and Illness. (1990). New York: Dell Publishing.

Wherever You Go, There You Are. (2005). New York: Hyperion.

Guided Mindfulness Meditation. (2005). Louisville, CO: Sounds True.

Mindfulness for Beginners. (2006). Louisville, CO: Sounds True.

Below we provide a few examples of mindfulness exercises that you could use, but we strongly recommend that you learn about mindfulness through reading, training and personal experience before facilitating these exercises.

Breathing mindfulness

Ask the participants to get comfortable. Then direct their attention to their breathing—to the breath entering and leaving their bodies. Encourage them not to change their breathing, but to let it continue effortlessly. Have them return their focus to their breath if they notice themselves getting distracted.

Listening mindfulness

Direct the participants to get comfortable and to begin by focusing on their breath. Ask them to notice any sounds they hear in the room, including the sounds of their body. Alternatively, you could have them listen to a piece of music, an instrument or anything that makes sound. It is not what they are listening to that matters, but rather that they practise actively listening. Encourage participants to return their focus to the sounds in the room (or the chosen auditory stimulus) whenever their mind wanders. Ask them to note what they notice during the exercise. After they finish this exercise, invite them to use this kind of focused attention when listening to others.

Body mindfulness

Tell the participants to get comfortable and to begin by focusing on their breath. Pass around a bottle of hand cream (or two bottles, for a larger group) and ask them to squeeze some onto their hands. Once everyone has done so, instruct them to rub the cream into their hands for about two minutes. Encourage them to focus closely on this experience, noticing how it feels physically and emotionally. Suggest that they return their focus to the cream and their hands if they notice themselves getting distracted.

RELAXATION EXERCISES

Relaxation exercises are particularly helpful for family members, who are often stressed, tense and anxious. There are many books that provide relaxation exercises, including the following:

Bourne, E.J. (2005). *The Anxiety and Phobia Workbook* (4th ed.). Oakland, CA: New Harbinger Publications.

Schiraldi, G.R. (1997). *Conquer Anxiety, Worry and Nervous Fatigue: A Guide to Greater Peace.* Ellicott City, MD: Chevron Publishing.

Below we provide some examples of relaxation exercises that you could use. Again, you should obtain knowledge of relaxation through reading, training and personal experience before using these exercises with the group.

Breathing relaxation

Tell the participants to get comfortable, and then ask them to put their hands on their abdomen. Guide them to notice their breathing and to try to allow their abdomen to expand with every inhalation, rather than their shoulders raising. Suggest that they gradually slow down their breathing. You may wish to guide them to count silently as they breathe (particularly as they exhale), or to focus on a calming word as they exhale.

Progressive muscle relaxation

Tell the participants to get comfortable. Ask them to tense the muscles in their toes on an in-breath and to hold the tension for a breath. Then, on an out-breath, have them relax these muscles. Encourage them to notice the tension leaving their toes. Continue this systematically through the various parts of the body (feet, calves and thighs up to shoulders, neck and face).

Guided imagery relaxation

Tell the participants to get comfortable, and then ask them to focus on their breathing. Guide them on a visual mental journey or help them visualize a relaxing scene. For instance, you could ask them to take a trip in which they are gently floating with the breeze or to picture themselves relaxing on a beach. Encourage them to use their imagination to experience the sensations of the place (e.g., the sound of the waves, the heat of the sun, the coolness of the breeze).

CHECK-INS AND CHECK-OUTS

Check-ins and check-outs at the start and end of sessions may be time-consuming. To avoid going over time, we suggest you stick to one of the following options:

· Ask the participants to share one thing that they did differently during the week.
· Ask them to share one thing that they learned about themselves during the week or during the session.
· Ask them to share in a few words how they are currently feeling.
· Ask them to indicate something that they want to learn more about.
· Ask them to state their reaction to something that occurred during the week or in the session.
· Ask them to share any questions or confusions that they have about material that was presented.

SPIRITUAL OR COGNITIVE EXERCISES

There are many spiritual or cognitive exercises that can help to encourage and guide family members. Participants themselves may suggest possible exercises, and you may accumulate examples from your own work. Below are two examples.

Serenity Prayer

Read aloud (or read together with the participants) the following portion of the Serenity Prayer. Give the participants a couple of minutes to think about the words and how the words relate to them.

God, grant me the serenity to accept the things I cannot change, the courage to change the things I can, and the wisdom to know the difference.

—Reinhold Niebuhr

NOTE: The Serenity Prayer is often associated with Alcoholics Anonymous, and for some people it may be associated with the Christian faith. If participants are uncomfortable with this prayer, you may wish not to use it, or to encourage participants to focus on its message rather than its origin.

The seven Cs

Read the "seven Cs," listed below. Give the participants a couple of minutes to think about the words and how the words relate to them.

I didn't *cause* it.
I can't *cure* it.
I can't *control* it.
I can take *care* of myself.
I can *communicate* my feelings.
I can make healthy *choices*.
I can *celebrate* being me.

—National Association for Children of Alcoholics (NACoA)

Inspirational quotations

We have included several helpful quotations in Module 17: Finding Hope. You can also find inspirational sayings in many books and on the Internet. Here are some examples.

Cook, J. (1993). *The Book of Positive Quotations*. Minneapolis, MN: Fairview Press.

Reader's Digest editors. (1997). *Quotable Quotes: Wit and Wisdom for All Occasions from America's Most Popular Magazine*. Pleasantville, NY: Reader's Digest.

Warner, C. (1992). *The Last Word: A Treasury of Women's Quotes*. Englewood Cliffs, NJ: Prentice Hall.

www.heartsandminds.org

www.motivationalquotes.com

Here are some examples of quotations you might use to open or close a session:

"The only way round is through." (Robert Frost)

"Although the world is full of suffering, it is also full of the overcoming of it." (Helen Keller)

"One doesn't discover new lands without consenting to lose sight of the shore for a very long time." (André Gide)

"In the choice between changing one's mind and proving there's no need to do so, most people get busy on the proof." (John Kenneth Galbraith)

"It is not the strongest of the species that survives, nor the most intelligent; it is the one most responsive to change." (Charles Darwin)

Implementing the program

The initial interview

We recommend that prior to providing the program, you interview each interested family member (if two or more members of the same family are seeking treatment, you can interview them together). The interview gives potential participants an opportunity to tell you about themselves and their situation, and allows you to discuss confidentiality, determine family members' eligibility, orient them to the program and discover their treatment needs.

CONFIDENTIALITY

At the start of the interview you should outline the limits of confidentiality and how confidentiality is ensured. In most jurisdictions, the client's confidentiality is protected unless there is a risk of harm (including harm caused by drinking and driving) to the client or others known to the client; a child is being abused or neglected; a client discloses having been sexually abused by a registered health care provider; or a client's file has been subpoenaed. In most agencies, client information is maintained securely, either electronically or in a locked filing cabinet.

HEARING THEIR STORY

Many family members have had few, if any, opportunities to share their story with others, and have a need to do so with a non-judgmental person. It is important to allow them time to talk about their experiences and their situation, and to provide supportive, validating responses. Allowing time for this during the interview allows potential participants to become more comfortable talking about their situation, which helps to prepare them for the group treatment. It also helps them to develop a connection and sense of trust with you, which will encourage their attendance at group sessions.

This portion of the interview should not be highly structured, but we encourage you to provide direction and containment if a person is becoming too emotionally vulnerable. We also recommend that you help family members focus on their strengths and coping resources, so they do not become overwhelmed with hopelessness at their situation. Praise them for their efforts at handling the situation and at coping, even if their methods have not proven successful.

Questions you might want to ask during this section include:
· What has brought you to seek treatment?
· How is your relationship with _____ [the person with a substance use problem]?
· How has _____'s substance use affected you, your relationship and others around you?
· What treatment have you or _____ received and what has been the outcome?
· What have you done to try to improve your situation?
· How have you coped with your situation?

DETERMINING ELIGIBILITY

Families CARE can be helpful to many family members of people who have substance use problems, but some people may not be ready for it or able to benefit from it, and for others the program might interfere with existing treatment. The following are exclusion criteria:
· substance use problems
· severe mental health problems
· risk of harm
· severe crisis.

Substance use problems

Some family members may themselves use substances to a greater or lesser extent. We recommend excluding family members who themselves have substance use problems, because they may feel uncomfortable when other group members express their negative feelings about a relative's substance use, and may not share the common desire of other group members for their relative to reduce his or her substance use. You will therefore need to ask family members about their own use, and determine if it is problematic. You may recommend that people not eligible for the program for this reason receive substance use treatment prior to participating in Families CARE.

Severe mental health problems

Some potential participants may be experiencing mental health problems, due perhaps in part to the stress of dealing with their relative who has a substance use problem. They may nonetheless be able to participate in Families CARE if the problem is mild to moderate and the person is relatively stable, or even if the problem is more severe but is being successfully treated elsewhere and is relatively stable. But for some family members with more severe mental problems that are not being treated and are not stabilized, the program may not be suitable. You will therefore need to determine the mental health and stability of family members, and may recommend that those with severe depression or anxiety, mania, psychosis or personality disorder receive mental health treatment before participating in Families CARE.

Risk of harm

Some family members may be at risk of harm, either from another person or from themselves. You should assess the risk to potential participants of abuse, violence, self-harm and suicide. If there is a risk of harm, you will need to ensure the person's safety by developing a safety plan (see Module 7: Staying Safe and Managing Crises) and, if necessary, contacting and involving the relevant authorities. If a person is experiencing or at risk of severe abuse, we advise referring him or her for appropriate treatment, such as services for people experiencing domestic violence. While people in these situations will not be able to participate in the program, they should be encouraged to join when their situation has stabilized.

Severe crisis

Many people affected by familial substance use experience regular crises, which may sometimes have the paradoxical benefit of prompting them to seek treatment. Further, it is a goal of Families CARE that participation will help family members to prevent and deal with crises better. Nonetheless, family members may at times be so distraught and preoccupied by a severe crisis that they would not be able to benefit from the program at the current time. We suggest that in such cases you provide them with support and assistance (or refer them if necessary) and reconsider them for the program when they or their situation is more stable.

ORIENTATION TO THE PROGRAM

Family members should be given a description of the treatment to enable them to make an informed decision about their participation, and to develop realistic expectations about treatment. We recommend that you provide the following information:

· program details: the time, location, length and number of sessions; the facilitators; the approximate number of participants; whether groups are observed or videotaped, etc.

· program components: the general format of sessions, the inclusion of home practice assignments, the policy about attendance, etc.

· program goals (explain to potential participants that the focus of the treatment is on them and their needs, rather than the functioning of the person who has a substance use problem):
  - to increase family members' knowledge about substance use and concurrent disorders, recovery and treatment
  - to improve family members' well-being through better coping, self-care, support, spirituality, grieving, management of emotions and stress, and finding hope
  - to improve family members' situations through enhancing safety, managing crises, problem solving, and attaining goals
  - to improve family members' relationships through more effective communication, limit setting, response and support

· program content: topics that may be addressed

· alternative treatment options: other relevant programs offered at your facility or agency, or in the community.

DETERMINING TREATMENT NEEDS

The pre-treatment survey (see Appendix 1 of the Introduction, page 21) allows family members to note their goals and expectations, and to identify what topics they hope to address during the program and what questions they want answered.

You should also determine if potential participants have special needs for which accommodations might be needed (e.g., physical disabilities, hearing or visual impairments, food allergies [if food is being provided], or issues with reading proficiency or fluency in English), or cultural or religious beliefs that may be pertinent to the treatment process.

Ensure that family members understand the process going forward (e.g., who to contact for support, the date and time of the next appointment). Reinforce them for having taken this first step in seeking treatment and support.

Recommended format for sessions

For sessions of two hours, we suggest the following format:
· Opening and announcements (5 min.)
· Check-in and review of last week's home practice (approx. 30 min.)
· Break (optional) (15 min.)
· Teaching and discussion (60 min.)
· Assignment of home practice (5 min.)
· Closing (5 min.).

These timings will need to be condensed for shorter sessions.

OPENING

An opening ritual or exercise provides structure, routine and safety to the group, as well as helping participants prepare to take part in the group. Appendix 2 of the Introduction (page 23) provides some examples of possible opening (and closing) exercises, though different facilitators may have their own approaches to opening and closing sessions.

ANNOUNCEMENTS

You will probably want to provide information on cancellations or changes to the group schedule, staff absences and any upcoming workshops or events that might interest the group members. Participants may also have announcements about their own upcoming absences or about relevant services or events.

CHECK-IN AND HOME PRACTICE REVIEW

Following the opening exercise and announcements, you will need to review the participants' home practice from the previous week. This review is crucial: people learn new skills by practising them in familiar environments such as at home, and the participants are more likely to do so if they know they will be sharing their home practice experiences in the group, and if they have the opportunity for feedback from the facilitators and the other participants about what they have done well and what they could have done differently. Research indicates a strong relationship between homework completion and positive outcomes (Scheel et al., 2004).

During this part of the session, each person should have time to speak about what he or she practised during the week, and to discuss any difficulties or positive experiences. Facilitators and the other participants can reinforce the importance of practising at home and help family members to recognize their accomplishments. You can also help with problem solving if anyone encountered obstacles.

Given that sessions will probably be time-limited, we do not recommend unstructured opening check-ins, which may become lengthy. If family members want to share their experiences at length, they may be better served in a support group.

BREAK

There are pros and cons to offering a break. Whether or not you decide to do so will probably depend on the length of your sessions. If you do decide to provide a break, it may be best to do so before beginning the teaching section. If there is no break, you may wish to provide refreshments and snacks during the group. A snack may serve as an added incentive for coming to the group, and can help people to concentrate better during the session.

TEACHING AND DISCUSSION

At this point, you will follow the module outlines presented in this manual. You may wish to use all the materials that are provided for a given module, or to select those most relevant to your group. Each module focuses on a different topic and skill, but you may wish to spend more than one session on certain modules.

HOME PRACTICE ASSIGNMENT

Next you will assign and explain the home practice based on the module you have covered. Usually, participants will need to decide what to do for their homework ahead of time. One option is to instruct them to write down what they plan to do and share it with the group, since a verbal commitment will increase the likelihood of their completing the assignment. Encourage participants to record what they practise during the week, so they can later refer back to their homework.

Some modules require participants to complete a reading or prepare something prior to the session. In order to let family members know about this, you will need to know which module you are doing next and whether it requires preparatory work at home.

If any participants have difficulty reading or writing in English, facilitators may need to adapt or verbally explain the homework exercises or readings, or (if the resources are available) have them translated into the person's first language.

CLOSING

As with the opening, we recommend that you end the session with some form of ritual, such as a brief relaxation, spiritual or mindfulness exercise (for examples, see Appendix 2 of the Introduction, page 23). At times, it may be helpful to relate the closing to the session's topic. For example:

· If you talked about self-care during the session, you could close by having family members listen to an inspirational poem on self-care, or listen to music, drink tea or eat something they enjoy.
· If you have completed a session on managing anxiety, you may wish to end with a relaxation exercise.
· If you have focused on supporting recovery, you may choose to end with the Serenity Prayer or the seven Cs (see Appendix 2 of the Introduction).

In this way, the closing exercise enables participants to practise what they have learned.

Dealing with common difficulties in facilitating groups

The therapists at CAMH's Family Addiction Service have developed experience over many years in dealing with various group challenges. Below we discuss some of the common difficulties that you may face and how we recommend dealing with them. Our recommendations should inform, but not take the place of, your own clinical judgment, as well as professional ethics and agency procedures.

A GROUP MEMBER ARRIVES IN CRISIS

If a person arrives early and in distress, we recommend that you ask to speak to him or her for a few minutes in private.

If a participant arrives in distress after the group has started, briefly assess whether the person wishes to discuss the crisis in the group, whether the crisis is relevant to the group and will not overwhelm the participants, and whether the issue can be dealt with easily. If so, set aside a brief period (e.g., five to 10 minutes) to discuss the crisis before moving into the regular group agenda. Since this is not a process group, the goal of the discussion should not be to process the crisis at length, but to validate and provide support to the person, and to help him or her become calm enough to focus on the group. You may offer to spend time with the person after the session to discuss the crisis in more detail and to help the person problem solve. During this discussion, you will need to assess the risk of harm to the participant or to others.

If the participant does not wish to discuss the crisis in the group, if the crisis is not relevant to the group or if it is too large to be dealt with in the group, you should suggest that the participant speak to you after the session. If, however, the person is too distressed and dysregulated to take part in the group, leave the group to further assess the situation. (If you are the only facilitator present, be brief and, if possible, call upon another therapist to help out so you can quickly return to the group.) The goal of this private meeting should be to help the person become calm enough to return to the group as soon as possible. You should also assess the risk of harm to the client or others. If anyone is at risk of harm, consult with other team members or with supervisors for guidance and support, following appropriate organizational and professional protocols. If the person is suicidal, if there is a risk of harm to others or if a child has been harmed, it may be necessary to breach confidentiality and contact the relevant authorities.

A GROUP MEMBER BECOMES EMOTIONALLY DYSREGULATED

We recommend that facilitators try to keep group members' emotions under reasonable control by providing adequate structure and containment, and at times limiting their emotional expression. Participants may nonetheless become dysregulated at times (e.g., crying inconsolably, shaking, yelling, swearing or even becoming violent). If this occurs, first ensure the safety of everyone involved, even if that means asking a person to leave the group. Once safety is ensured, validate the person's emotions and ask what would be help him or her to become calmer. You may provide suggestions, such as focusing on breathing or counting, distracting himself or herself, or having something to drink or eat. Do not ask process or deepening questions, as they are likely to increase the person's distress.

If the person is unable to control his or her emotions, you might suggest that he or she leave the group temporarily to calm down, for example by walking around, going to the bathroom, washing his or her face, or getting a drink. If you are concerned about the participant's safety, one of the facilitators should accompany the person. If the participant leaves the group alone, a facilitator may follow up after a short time by checking how the person is doing and inviting him or her to return (people who become emotionally dysregulated in front of others often feel exposed, embarrassed or ashamed, and may find it difficult to return to the group).

A GROUP MEMBER DISCLOSES INFORMATION ABOUT ONGOING ABUSE OR IMMINENT RISK OF HARM

If a group member discloses his or her own current abuse or the risk of harm, we recommend that you do not process the person's experience, but focus on developing a safety plan. Given how frequently abuse occurs in relationships affected by problematic substance use, this issue is important for everyone in your group to consider. Since other participants may have dealt with this issue themselves, they may be able to provide valuable support and feedback. In developing a safety plan, you should identify triggers and warning signs for violence, and help the person decide on possible plans of action should these warning signs occur. Emphasize to the participants that their safety is a priority and that should it be compromised, they should act immediately to protect themselves. If necessary, you may offer the family member an opportunity to discuss the situation in more detail after the session.

If a group member discloses the risk of harm to another adult, you will need to discuss how he or she can help this person become safe. You will need to assess whether confidentiality will need to be breached to ensure the person's safety. Consult with other team members and supervisors in deciding how to proceed.

If a group member discloses harm or the risk of harm to a child, you will need to discuss the situation with the person privately and will need to determine whether child welfare authorities should be contacted. Again, you should consult with other team members and supervisors in deciding how to proceed. If you decide to contact child welfare authorities, we encourage you to try to involve the disclosing participant in making the call.

A GROUP MEMBER MAKES AN INAPPROPRIATE COMMENT

If a group member makes an inappropriate comment, we recommend that you intervene. Depending on the type of comment, you may state that not everyone might agree with or feel comfortable with the statement. You can allow other participants to respond, but we would caution against a long processing of the event. You may take the opportunity to revisit the group guidelines (see Module 1, page 42), and remind the participants of the need for these norms to ensure safety in the group. You may also choose to speak after the session with the person who made the inappropriate comment to determine whether any other issues need to be addressed.

If a participant tells you after a session that he or she was hurt or offended by something said in the group, you should take the opportunity at the next session to remind the group of the rules and norms and emphasize the importance of safety within the group, without referring to the specific incident.

GROUP MEMBERS ARE IN CONFLICT

If a disagreement between two or more participants escalates to an inappropriate level, you should intervene to end the conflict. If a person is unable or unwilling to stop, you may ask the person to take a break from the group for a few minutes. Then, with all participants present, remind them of the group rules and norms, and discuss appropriate ways of managing differing viewpoints.

If the conflict continues, you might meet after the session with those involved to try to resolve the issue or obtain an agreement on how to manage the issue in future sessions. If the conflict cannot be resolved, you may have to offer those involved an alternative group or treatment.

GROUP MEMBERS CONTRIBUTE UNEQUALLY

In any group, some members will talk more and some less. However, if one or more participants talk excessively during the group, sidetrack the discussion, prevent others from contributing, dominate the discussion or reveal too much personal information, you will need to intervene to restore balance in the group. If a person is being wordy or tangential, you may need to interrupt and redirect him or her to the task at hand. Explain that everyone needs to have a turn speaking, and encourage others to contribute. If necessary, be more structured and task-focused in leading the group. For example, avoid open-ended or personal questions that could allow for lengthy sharing.

If one or more group members are frequently quiet, be sensitive to their need to listen, but also give them the time and space to contribute. You may need to pause for longer after asking questions to allow them the time to volunteer an answer. It may also be helpful to ask everyone to share by going around in a circle.

Reference

Scheel, M.J., Hanson, W.E. & Razzhavaikina, T.I. (2004). The process of recommending homework in psychotherapy: A review of therapist delivery methods, client acceptability, and factors that affect compliance. *Psychotherapy: Theory, Research, Practice, Training, 41* (1), 38–55.

Starting out

OBJECTIVES

· to present the goals and format of the group
· to determine the topics to be covered, based on group members' needs
· to establish guidelines for participating in the group
· to facilitate group members' sharing about their situation
· to accomplish the objectives of an additional module chosen for this session

HANDOUTS

Pre-treatment survey (Appendix 1 of the Introduction, p. 21)
Handouts for the additional module presented in this session.

SESSION OUTLINE

· Introduction (approx. 5 min.)
· Group guidelines (approx. 5 min.)
· Purpose of the group (approx. 5 min.)
· Group introductions (approx. 30 min.)
· Teaching and discussion (45–60 min.)
· Assigning of next week's home practice (approx. 5 min.)
· Closing (approx. 5 min.)

Introduction

▶ **As group members arrive, distribute the pre-treatment survey (Appendix 1 of the Introduction to this manual) to anyone who did not complete it during the initial screening and assessment session. Ask that they complete and return the survey before the group starts.**

Introduce yourself and any other facilitators to the group and briefly present your credentials and experience.

Group guidelines

Explain that the facilitators hold in confidence what is said in the group, and encourage the group members to maintain each others' confidentiality as well.

Outline the methods of ensuring confidentiality and the limits of confidentiality required by your agency. For example, at CAMH, we maintain all client documents in a record to which only clinicians and the client have access. If we discuss a client, we do so in a secure room only with members of our team; or, if we need to consult about a client with someone outside of our team, we do not give any personal identifying information. We must break confidentiality only if we become aware that a client is at risk of harming himself or herself or others (including a client who is or will be driving while intoxicated), that someone has been sexually abused by a registered health professional, or that a child is being harmed or is at risk of harm; or when a client's file has been subpoenaed.

Encourage group members to be open and honest about their situation and struggles, including their anger and frustration. At the same time, request that they be respectful in how they speak about the absent family member with a substance use problem. Explain that the purpose of the group is to help them cope and relate more effectively with that person, not to spend the time denigrating the person.

Encourage group members to be open and honest about their opinions, but to respect others' opinions as well. Remind them that there is often no single right or wrong way to deal with their situation.

Emphasize the importance of attending all sessions. If the group members cannot attend a session, they should call ahead to let the facilitators know.

Stress the importance of punctuality and note the effects of lateness on themselves, the group as a whole and the facilitators.

Inform group members that it is up to them whether they participate actively in the group and do homework between sessions, but encourage them to try to get the most out of the program. Emphasize that practising the material is the most effective way of making changes.

Purpose of the group

Tell the participants that the main goals of the group are:
· to learn how to take better care of themselves
· to increase their sense of control within their situation
· to get support from and to learn from others in similar situations
· to learn specific skills for coping and for managing feelings
· to learn how to respond more effectively and healthily to the person with a substance use problem, and how to support his or her recovery
· to improve their situation by problem solving and making changes
· to learn how to help children affected by familial substance use.

▶ **Hand out a schedule of topics to be covered.**

If you haven't decided on the schedule, tell the group members that you will give them a schedule next week.

Group introductions

Ask the group members to introduce themselves and to talk *briefly* about their situation, what brought them to the group and what they hope to gain from the group. Explain that over the weeks, they will have many opportunities to share with the group and do not need to give their entire story during this session. Observe and reinforce common themes that emerge as group members share.

Teaching and discussion

Choose a module to use in this section. We recommend that you begin with one of the following modules, which are less threatening and emotionally involving

than others (see Choosing Modules, page 14):
· Module 2: Understanding Substance Use Problems and Their Effect on Families
· Module 3: Taking Care of Yourself
· Module 4: Finding Support
· Module 5: Managing Stress.

Home practice

Assign and explain the homework based on the module that you chose to cover in this session.

Understanding substance use problems and their effect on families

OBJECTIVES

· to provide information on substance use problems and concurrent disorders
· to validate the effect of a relative's substance use problem on the group member
· to provide a safe environment in which group members can share their experiences
· to encourage group members to pay attention to how they are coping with the effects of their relative's substance use, and to increase coping efforts that are helping

HANDOUTS

2-1: Substance Use Problems: A Continuum
2-2: The Biopsychosocial Model of Substance Use Problems
2-3: Coping with the Effects of Substance Use

SESSION OUTLINE

· Opening and announcements (approx. 5 min.)
· Check-in and review of last week's home practice (approx. 30 min.)
· Teaching and discussion (approx. 60 min.)

· Assigning of next week's home practice (approx. 5 min.)

· Closing (approx. 5 min.)

Teaching and discussion

▶ **Distribute or turn to Handout 2-1: Substance Use Problems.**

Briefly present the continuum of substance use problems, from experimentation to dependence. Explain that the term "addiction" has been defined in many ways and used in many contexts; it is often used to describe behaviour that people have difficulty controlling (e.g., drinking alcohol, eating, spending money). Emphasize that when we speak about addiction, we are speaking primarily about the diagnoses of substance abuse and substance dependence. Explain that substance dependence is a more severe form of addiction than substance abuse.

It is useful to discuss the substance use problems that participants report in their relative within a larger framework of prevalence statistics. Here are some recent statistics that you may wish to share with group members.

According to the Canadian Community Health Survey (Statistics Canada, 2002), in which 37,000 Canadians (excluding those who were homeless, on Indian reserves, in institutions, in remote areas or in the Canadian Armed Forces) were interviewed:

· 77 per cent reported that they had drunk alcohol in the past 12 months.

· 35 per cent reported that they had engaged in at least one episode of heavy drinking (five or more drinks on a single occasion), of whom 48 per cent reported doing so at least once a month.

· 2.6 per cent reported symptoms consistent with alcohol dependence.

With regard to illicit drug use:

· 13 per cent reported that they had used illicit drugs in the past 12 months (10 per cent had used marijuana and two per cent had used other illicit drugs). Of this group, 32 per cent reported using at least once a week. Illicit drug use was more common among men, with 16 per cent of men and nine per cent of women having used illicit drugs in the past 12 months.

· 0.8 per cent reported symptoms consistent with drug dependence.

The survey found that 600,000 Canadians were dependent on alcohol and nearly 200,000 on illicit drugs.

Note that these statistics do not include problematic use of or dependence on prescription drugs.

Ask the group members what point on the substance use continuum their relative is at (e.g., experimentation, abuse).

CONCURRENT SUBSTANCE USE AND MENTAL HEALTH PROBLEMS

In the most formal sense, *concurrent disorders* (or co-occurring disorders) are defined as the presence of at least one diagnosed mental health disorder and at least one diagnosed substance use disorder. A person with concurrent disorders may have more than one disorder simultaneously, or may have a lifetime history of concurrent disorders (i.e., he or she meets the diagnostic criteria of at least one mental health disorder and at least one substance use disorder at different times).

Less formally, the term is used to describe co-occurring substance use and mental health problems, whether or not a formal diagnosis has been made.

Point out that concurrent disorders are often not diagnosed, primarily because it is hard to conduct a mental health assessment of a person who is or has been using substances: the effects of substance intoxication or withdrawal can mask, exacerbate or mimic the symptoms of mental health disorders, making it difficult to determine the existence of a mental health disorder. Nonetheless, because the rate of concurrent disorders is so high, it is important that clinicians, clients and family members consider the possibility.

You may also explain that another reason for failure to detect concurrent disorders is that a person may have either a mental health or a substance use disorder that is subclinical. In other words, the person shows symptoms of both disorders, but does not meet the full diagnostic criteria for both. Given that our diagnostic system is categorical rather than dimensional (i.e., a person either fits the criteria fully or doesn't fit them at all), people who have less severe problems may not be diagnosed. They may nonetheless have concurrent problems that warrant consideration and attention.

Some examples of concurrent substance use and mental health problems include the following:
· alcohol problems and depression
· problematic amphetamine use and an eating disorder
· cocaine use and borderline personality disorder
· problematic morphine use and bipolar disorder
· problematic alcohol use and social anxiety disorder.

If a person has either a mental health or a substance use disorder, there is a greater likelihood of the person having the other problem as well. One study (Statistics Canada, 2002) found that:

- 16.1 per cent of people diagnosed with any mental disorder during their lifetime experienced a substance use problem some time in the preceding year
- 27.5 per cent of those identified with a current alcohol problem will also have a mental illness at some point in their lifetime
- 38.3 per cent of those with a current substance use problem other than an alcohol problem will also have a mental health disorder at some point in their lifetime
- the risk of mental illness increased with the severity of the substance use disorder (for instance, people with substance use problems were at twice the risk of meeting the criteria for lifetime mental illness, while people with substance dependence were at four times the normal risk of meeting the criteria for lifetime mental illness compared to the general population.

Ask the group members if their relative has been diagnosed with or is showing symptoms of a concurrent mental health problem.

Interaction between substance use and mental health problems

The relationship between concurrent mental health and substance use problems is complicated and hard to disentangle. The following are some of the ways that mental health and substance use problems can interact:

- Mental health and substance use problems can both be triggered by the same factor(s) (e.g., a traumatic event, an emotionally sensitive temperament).
- Mental health problems can be triggered or exacerbated by the presence of substance use problems (e.g., the development of depression following period of substance use, in part because of losses the person experienced during substance use).
- Substance use problems can be triggered or exacerbated by the presence of mental health problems (e.g., repeated attempts to self-medicate anxiety using alcohol).

Even when one problem was clearly present before the other, the problems may interact, and the relationship between them may change over time.

For more information

For more information on this topic for group members and for yourself, please refer to:

O'Grady, C.P. & Skinner, W.J.W. (2007). *A Family Guide to Concurrent Disorders*. Toronto: Centre for Addiction and Mental Health.

O'Grady, C.P. & Skinner, W.J.W. (2007). *Partnering with Families Affected by Concurrent Disorders: Facilitators' Guide*. Toronto: Centre for Addiction and Mental Health.

Both these resources are available at:
www.camh.net/About_Addiction_Mental_Health/Concurrent_Disorders/
CD_priority_projects.html.

SIGNS OF SUBSTANCE USE PROBLEMS

▶ **Ask the group members to list the signs of substance use they have noticed in their relative. Write their responses on a blackboard, whiteboard or flipchart.**

Many of these signs may also be indications of a co-occurring mental health problem. Here are some examples:
· denial, minimization or rationalization of use
· loss of control of use
· preoccupation with use
· increased need for money
· change in appearance, friends, personality and routine
· increased or decreased sociability
· decreased or impaired communication
· decreased productivity and responsibility
· decreased trustworthiness and reliability
· impaired concentration, judgment and long-term thinking
· compromised values, ethics and standards
· increased social, legal, financial and work-related problems
· increased physical symptoms and health problems
· increased mental health problems
· increased engagement in high-risk behaviours.

WHY DO PEOPLE USE SUBSTANCES?

Ask the group members why they believe that their relative started using a substance and/or continues using substances.

▶ **Write their responses on a blackboard, whiteboard or flipchart. Add any of the following reasons that they have not mentioned.**

Substance use:
· helps the person avoid dealing with problems
· helps the person feel better
· helps the person cope
· increases the person's sense of confidence

· helps the person do something he or she would not otherwise be able to do
· helps the person fit in with peers
· increases the person's status within a group
· communicates a message to others.

Explain that people typically begin using substances because it is pleasurable or reinforcing in some way, even if a substance's ability to provide reinforcement changes over time (e.g., drinking alcohol initially helped a person to sleep, but no longer does so).

The biopsychosocial model

▶ **Distribute or turn to Handout 2-2: The Biopsychosocial Model of Substance Use Problems.**

Explain that there is no simple reason why people develop problems with substance use. Most of the models that try to explain substance use problems include a variety of factors. Use the handout to describe the different types of factors presented in the biopsychosocial model.

Parents may wonder if they have contributed to their adult child's substance use problems. You could gently say that they may indeed have played a *small* role in their child developing such a problem, but that many other factors would also have contributed. Explain that the model is not exhaustive, but that it provides examples of what research tells us are risk factors for developing substance use problems.

EFFECTS OF SUBSTANCE USE ON THE FAMILY

▶ **Distribute or turn to Handout 2-3: Coping with the Effects of Substance Use, and ask the group members to fill in the "Effects" column. Write their responses on a blackboard, whiteboard or flipchart.**

Below are examples of the effects on family members of a relative's substance use problems that you may hear from group members, and from what we know from research:
· denial or minimization of the problem
· preoccupation with the person using substances
· shifting and unpredictable roles within relationships
· the tendency to rescue and protect the person using substances
· difficulties fulfilling regular responsibilities (e.g., work)

· conflict and deterioration of family relationships
· attempts to monitor, control and change the person using substances
· increased confusion, anxiety, depression, distress, grief, anger, shame, guilt or helplessness
· loss of trust in the person using substances
· withdrawal and social isolation
· loss of security or safety (e.g., financial security or physical safety)
· abuse and exploitation by the person using substances
· self-neglect and burnout.

Coping with these effects

▶ **Ask the group members to complete the "Coping" column in Handout 2-3. List some of their coping efforts on a blackboard, whiteboard or flipchart.**

Praise clients for their *efforts* at coping, even if their *methods* have not been healthy or helpful. Go over the list on the board and ask which efforts have been helpful and useful.

If this is the first session, emphasize that the group sessions will help them learn to deal more effectively with the person who has a substance use problem.

Home practice

▶ **Turn to Handout 2-3: Coping with the Effects of Substance Use.**

Ask the group members to identify one method they have used to cope with the effects of their relative's substance use that was helpful, and to continue using this strategy during the week.

For more information

For more information, please refer to the following:

American Psychiatric Association. (1994). *Diagnostic and Statistical Manual of Mental Disorders* (4th ed.). Washington, DC: Author.

Avenevoli, S., Conway, K.P. & Merikangas, K.R. (2005). Familial risk factors for substance use disorders. In J. Hudson & R. Rapee (Eds.), *Psychopathology and the Family* (pp. 167–192). New York: Elsevier Science.

Butler, R. & Bauld, L. (2005). The parents' experience: Coping with drug use in the family. *Drugs: Education, Prevention and Policy, 12* (1), 35–45.

Marsh, A. & Dale, A. (2005). Risk factors for alcohol and other drug disorders: A review. *Australian Psychologist, 40* (2), 73–80.

Mayes, L.C. & Suchman, N.E. (2006). Developmental pathways to substance abuse. In D. Cicchetti & D.J. Cohen (Eds.), *Developmental Psychopathology, Vol. 3: Risk, Disorder, and Adaptation* (2nd ed.; pp. 599–619). New York: John Wiley & Sons.

O'Grady, C.P. & Skinner, W.J.W. (2007). *A Family Guide to Concurrent Disorders.* Toronto: Centre for Addiction and Mental Health.

Statistics Canada. (2002). *Canadian Community Health Survey, Cycle 1.2.* Ottawa: Author.

Tarter, R.E., Vanyukov, M., Giancola, P., Dawes, M., Blackson, T., Mezzich, A. et al. (1999). Etiology of early age onset substance use disorder: A maturational perspective. *Development and Psychopathology, 11* (4), 657–683.

Velleman, R., Bennett, G., Miller, T., Orford, J., Rigby, K. & Tod, A. (1993). The families of problem drug users: A study of 50 close relatives. *Addiction, 88,* 1281–1289.

Zucker, R.A. (2006). Alcohol use and the alcohol use disorders: A developmental-biopsychosocial systems formulation covering the life course. In D. Cicchetti & D.J. Cohen (Eds.), *Developmental Psychopathology, Vol 3: Risk, Disorder, and Adaptation* (2nd ed.; pp. 620–656). New York: John Wiley & Sons.

Reference

Statistics Canada. (2002). *Canadian Community Health Survey, Cycle 1.2.* Ottawa: Author.

Substance use problems

Substance Use Problems: A Continuum

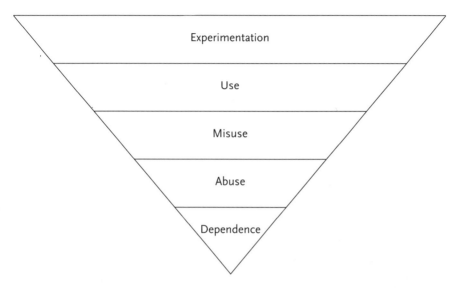

DEFINING SUBSTANCE ABUSE AND DEPENDENCE

Substance abuse

People who abuse substances regularly may have ongoing serious problems without being dependent on the substance. Some of these problems are:

· inability to fulfil responsibilities (e.g., being absent from work, doing poorly in school or neglecting duties at home)

· dangerous use (e.g., using substances in physically dangerous situations, such as when driving a car)

· legal problems (e.g., being arrested for disorderly conduct following substance use)

· social and family problems (e.g., arguing with family members about being intoxicated).

If one or more of these problems have a significant impact on a person's life, the person may be diagnosed with a substance abuse disorder.

Substance dependence

People who are dependent on substances have major physical, mental and behaviour problems that can have serious effects on their lives. Some of the signs of substance dependence are:

· tolerance: the need to use larger and larger amounts of the substance to get the desired effect, such as intoxication
· withdrawal: having unpleasant symptoms if substance use stops; continued substance use with the same or similar drugs to avoid or reduce withdrawal symptoms
· desire to cut down or quit: many unsuccessful attempts to reduce or stop using the substance
· time investment: a great deal of time spent getting the substance, using it or recovering from its effects
· retreat from usual activities: giving up or reducing work, social or recreational activities, and withdrawing from family and friends to use the substance privately or to spend more time with friends who use substances
· ongoing use: substance use continues despite the negative effects.

If three or more of these problems are ongoing during a 12-month period, a person may be diagnosed with a substance dependence disorder.

USE OF ALCOHOL AND OTHER DRUGS IN CANADA

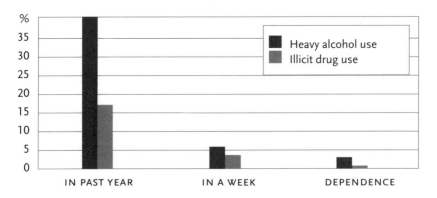

Source: Statistics Canada. (2002). *Canadian Community Health Survey, Cycle 1.2.* Ottawa: Author.
Interviewers asked 37,000 Canadians about their use of alcohol or other drugs during the past 12 months.

The biopsychosocial model of substance use problems

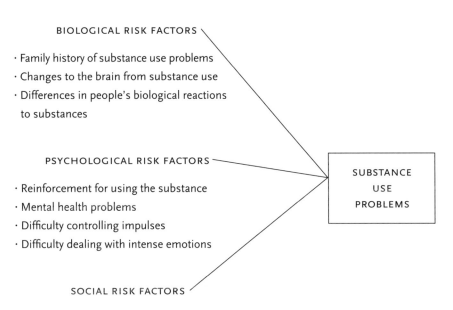

BIOLOGICAL RISK FACTORS

· Family history of substance use problems
· Changes to the brain from substance use
· Differences in people's biological reactions
  to substances

PSYCHOLOGICAL RISK FACTORS

· Reinforcement for using the substance
· Mental health problems
· Difficulty controlling impulses
· Difficulty dealing with intense emotions

SUBSTANCE
USE
PROBLEMS

SOCIAL RISK FACTORS

· Societal acceptance and glorification of substance use
· Peer pressure
· Lack of social support (including being single)
· Difficult or traumatic past or current family experiences
· Adjustment difficulties due to immigration
  and settlement

Coping with the effects of substance use

One person's substance use can affect many people. We would like you to think about the effects of your relative's substance use on you and other people in the family, and how you have been coping with these effects.

	EFFECTS OF THE SUBSTANCE USE	COPING EFFORTS
On you		
On your family		

Taking care of yourself

OBJECTIVES

· to help group members shift their focus from the person with a substance use problem to themselves and their own needs
· to emphasize the importance of self-care
· to encourage group members to identify ways in which they can take better care of themselves
· to help participants overcome barriers to self-care

HANDOUTS

3-1: Self-Care
3-2: Self-Care Strategies
3-3: My Self-Care Strategies
3-4: Practising Self-Care

SESSION OUTLINE

· Opening and announcements (approx. 5 min.)
· Check-in and review of last week's home practice (approx. 30 min.)
· Teaching and discussion (approx. 60 min.)
· Assigning of next week's home practice (approx. 5 min.)
· Closing (approx. 5 min.)

CLIENT PREPARATION

At the previous session, ask the group members to identify something (e.g., an activity) that brings them meaning, joy, fulfilment or restoration, and to bring with them a token that reflects this aspect of their lives (e.g., someone who enjoys the company of a pet could bring in a photo of the pet; someone who gets fulfilment from art could bring in artwork).

Teaching and discussion

IMPORTANCE OF NURTURING ONESELF

Explain that having someone in the family with a substance use problem takes a toll on the rest of the family. If you have not already done so in a previous session, you may want to spend some time briefly discussing the ways in which families are affected.

State that one effect of being in a relationship with such a person is the tendency of partners, other relatives and friends to neglect their own needs.

Ask the group members why they believe it is important to care for themselves. For example, people who take care of their own health are likely to be:

· less vulnerable emotionally and physically
· more mindful and aware of themselves emotionally, physically, spiritually and socially
· more balanced within their relationships
· more able to endure being in a long-term relationship with someone uses substances (to emphasize this challenge, you could liken this long-term relationship to a marathon)
· less preoccupied with the other person's substance use
· more able to make wise decisions and to respond effectively within the relationship
· a healthier support to their partners, other family members and children (you could use the following analogy: when parents are travelling on an airplane, they are directed first to put on their own oxygen masks before helping their children to do so).

▶ **Distribute or turn to Handout 3-1: Self-Care.**

Go over each of the points briefly.

SELF-CARE ACTIVITIES

Ask the group members to share something about their life that brings them meaning, joy, fulfilment or restoration. If they have brought in a token representing this aspect of their life, ask them to share it with the group (see "Client Preparation"). Ask the group members:

· how they feel during and after engaging in this activity or aspect of their life
· how much time they spend on it
· if the amount of time they spend has changed over the years
· how much time they would *like* to spend on this activity or aspect of their life.

▶ **Distribute or turn to Handout 3-2: Self-Care Strategies.**

Suggest that the participants use this handout as a resource to help them think of how to take care of themselves. Encourage them to add other examples to the list.

Explain that even when the person using substances is not doing well, it is still important for the "healthy" family members to look after themselves and pursue their own interests, hobbies or activities. Talk about the positive effects of self-care activities (e.g., relaxation, play, diversion, laughter, sleep, eating) on one's body, mind, emotions and spirit. Explain that when we do not care for ourselves adequately, we are vulnerable to poor physical and emotional health.

If the examples the group members give are activities they can do *with* their relative, tell them that this is great for their relationship with the person, but perhaps less so for their own care. Talk about why they might want to engage in some self-care activities on their own. People with substance use problems are often inconsistent and unreliable, so it may be difficult for group members to count on their presence and positive involvement in an activity. Activities that should be nurturing, fulfilling and pleasurable might not happen at all, or might result in conflict if the person who uses substances is included in them.

Barriers to self-care

Discuss what gets in the way of group members caring for themselves or engaging in pleasurable activities.

The following are examples of barriers to self-care (you may note these if participants have not already mentioned them):
· lack of awareness of one's own needs
· preoccupation with the person who has a substance use problem
· having many responsibilities
· putting others' needs before one's own
· guilt about spending time and money taking care of oneself
· difficulty in managing time
· anxiety about the consequences for the person with a substance use problem, if you were to engage in self-care.

Discuss with the group ways to overcome the barriers to self-care that they have identified.

▶ **Distribute or turn to Handout 3-3: My Self-Care Strategies. Give participants about five minutes to complete the handout.**

Then ask them to share with the group what they have written.

Home practice

▶ **Distribute or turn to Handout 3-4: Practising Self-Care.**

Ask the participants to complete this handout at home. Suggest that every day
they engage in an activity that is nurturing and that gives them pleasure and/or
fulfilment. Ask them to notice how the activity affects their mood. If they are
already involved in activities that are nurturing, pleasurable and/or fulfilling,
suggest that they continue them or do more of them. Although it is important
that group members engage in some positive activities with their relative,
encourage them to do at least some self-care activities on their own.

Self-care

Seek social support

Engage in rest, relaxation and recreation

Let go of responsibility, guilt and anxiety

Feel and accept emotions

Commit to taking care of yourself daily

Allow yourself to experience love, joy, pride, peace, beauty and wonder

Respond to your physical, emotional, social and spiritual needs

Enjoy life

WHY SELF-CARE?

Taking care of your own health allows you to be:

· more healthy—physically, emotionally, spiritually, socially and in your relationships

· better able to respond to and support a relative with a substance use problem

· better able to parent and support children affected by familial substance use.

Self-care strategies

SELF-CARE ACTIVITIES

PERSONAL

Taking a bath	Sipping tea	Getting regular and
Getting a massage	Keeping a journal	sufficient sleep
Applying body lotion	Gardening	Enjoying a hobby
Getting a manicure or	Watching a movie	Taking a vacation
pedicure	Doing a relaxation	Buying a new outfit
Getting a haircut	exercise	Practising mindfulness
Exercising	Reading a good book	Praying
Practising yoga	Listening to music	Writing poetry
Going for a walk	Playing music	Doing athletics
Eating a good meal	Doing art	Going for a swim
Eating a favourite food	Building or constructing	Composing music
Lighting candles	something	Spending time in nature

SOCIAL

Spending time with family	Contacting a long-lost	Joining an exercise class
or friends	friend	Playing in a band or
Spending time with pets	Joining a yoga class	ensemble
Talking to family	Asking for support or help	Singing in a choir
Talking to friends	Taking a vacation with	Exercising with a friend
Going out for a meal	friends or family	Going camping
Going out for	Taking a course	
entertainment	Going back to school	
Writing a letter	Attending church, syna-	
Playing a sport	gogue, mosque, etc.	

PROFESSIONAL SUPPORT

Becoming educated about	Attending workshops	Talking to a spiritual
addiction	Obtaining mental health	leader
Attending a support or	treatment.	Receiving counselling
therapy group	Obtaining medical care	Reading self-help books

My self-care strategies

What activities am I doing that are enjoyable, nurturing and/or fulfilling?	
What other activities could I do that would be enjoyable, nurturing and/or fulfilling?	
What gets in the way of taking care of myself?	
How can I take better care of myself?	

Practising self-care

Engage in an activity every day that is pleasurable, nurturing or fulfilling.
Record the activity and how you felt before, during and after doing it.

MONDAY ACTIVITY

Feelings before:

Feelings during:

Feelings after:

TUESDAY ACTIVITY

Feelings before:

Feelings during:

Feelings after:

WEDNESDAY ACTIVITY

Feelings before:

Feelings during:

Feelings after:

THURSDAY ACTIVITY

Feelings before:

Feelings during:

Feelings after:

FRIDAY ACTIVITY
Feelings before:
Feelings during:
Feelings after:

SATURDAY ACTIVITY
Feelings before:
Feelings during:
Feelings after:

SUNDAY ACTIVITY
Feelings before:
Feelings during:
Feelings after:

Finding support

OBJECTIVES

· to help group members recognize the importance of finding and accessing
  support
· to help group members identify and overcome barriers to finding and
  accessing support

HANDOUTS

4-1: My Support System
4-2: Recognizing and Accessing Support

SESSION OUTLINE

· Opening and announcements (approx. 5 min.)
· Check-in and review of last week's home practice (approx. 30 min.)
· Teaching and discussion (approx. 60 min.)
· Assigning of next week's home practice (approx. 5 min.)
· Closing (approx. 5 min.)

Teaching and discussion

FINDING SUPPORT

▶ **Distribute or turn to Handout 4-1: My Support System, and Handout 4-2: Recognizing and Accessing Support. Ask the group members to take five minutes to complete Handout 4-1 and the first and third questions in Handout 4-2.**

Helpful support

Support can come from a variety of sources (e.g., neighbours, family members, friends, colleagues, managers, teachers, therapists, case workers, agencies, religious or faith communities, cultural leaders). Ask the group members:
· what kind of support they have received in dealing with the person who has a substance use problem
· how the support has been helpful to them.

▶ **Write the responses on a blackboard, whiteboard or flipchart.**

Researchers have consistently found a positive association between the quality of people's support and their health, well-being and/or recovery. Discuss with the group the importance of getting social support.

Unhelpful support

Ask how support has been *unhelpful* to them.

▶ **Write the responses on a blackboard, whiteboard or flipchart.**

The following distinction between helpful and unhelpful support was described by a team of researchers in England (Copello et al., 2000, page 337), who use the terms "supportive" and "unsupportive" (you may choose to present this information or use it to add to the lists that have been generated by group members):

A supportive other is someone who:
· is aware and knows about the problem
· is available to listen and understand
· is non-judgmental and accepting
· does not take sides
· is sensitive in knowing when to give advice
· offers material help
· offers help in accessing support services.

An unsupportive other is someone who:
- encourages substance misuse by the [person who uses substances]
- is uninvolved in the situation
- is uninformed about the situation
- is condemning of the situation
- is harsh in his or her attitude toward the [person who uses substances]
- gives unhelpful advice.

OVERCOMING BARRIERS TO SUPPORT

Ask the group members what led them to seek support. Praise them for having called an agency, for attending workshops or information seminars, for meeting with a therapist and/or for having joined this group. Ask if they had to combat any beliefs, feelings or behaviours related to asking for support before they did so.

Ask the participants what they believe has gotten in the way of their seeking support from others.

▶ **Write the responses on a blackboard, whiteboard or flipchart.**

After the discussion, try to group as many responses as possible into the categories of 1. independence (self-sufficiency) and isolation, and 2. stigma and shame. Here are some examples of possible responses that fall into each category:

INDEPENDENCE AND ISOLATION
- being unable to acknowledge to others that you need support
- believing that acknowledging needs or asking for help is a sign of weakness
- believing that you must manage alone
- believing that what happens in the family should be dealt with in the family
- believing that your family is different (perhaps culturally) and so cannot receive help from others
- not wanting to burden others with your problems
- not having close relationships with others within or outside the family
- not having time to spend with others
- not believing that professional resources might be helpful
- not knowing where to go for support or help.

STIGMA AND SHAME

· the shame felt by the person using substances, and his or her desire for secrecy
· one's own shame about the situation and the relationship
· fear of criticism, exclusion and judgment by others
· previous negative experiences of disclosing the situation (i.e., being judged or blamed oneself, or the person using substances being judged or blamed)
· experiences of discrimination by others
· mistrust of others
· negative messages or attitudes about people with substance use problems or people who are in a relationship with them
· cultural norms against admitting problems and seeking professional support.

Ask the group members:

· how to challenge beliefs about self-sufficiency and independence
· how to overcome isolation that is not due to stigma.

Then ask the group members to define stigma (*stigma* refers to negative attitudes about and treatment of certain groups of people, such as those with substance use problems).

Inform the group members that the person with a substance use problem is not the only one who may experience stigma. Explain that "courtesy stigma" refers to negative attitudes about and treatment of people who are related to someone with a substance use problem.

Ask the participants for examples of stigma that they have experienced. Ask them how they believe that they could challenge this stigma. Explain that one way to reduce stigma is by breaking the secrecy and beginning to talk to others about your experiences relating to someone with a substance use problem. Acknowledge the bravery that it takes to challenge stigma.

ACCESSING PROFESSIONAL SUPPORT

Ask the group members to share information about any other services that they have accessed and found helpful.

▶ **Distribute a list of community services and professional resources (e.g., counselling services, support groups, stress reduction or meditation classes) that could be helpful to the participants.**

Instruct them on ways to find services. For example, in Toronto, individuals can dial 211 or access www.211toronto.ca.

Home practice

▶ **Distribute or turn to Handout 4-2: Recognizing and Accessing Support.**

Before the group members leave, ask them to answer all the questions except the final one. Then ask them to discuss how they will increase their support system in the upcoming week. Encourage them to follow through with their plan as a homework assignment. Emphasize that they have already begun to increase their social support by attending this group.

Reference

Copello, A., Orford, J., Velleman, R., Templeton, L. & Krishnan, M. (2000). Methods for reducing alcohol and drug related family harm in non-specialist settings. *Journal of Mental Health, 9* (3), 329–343.

My support system

Label each circle with a person or service that is part of your support network. Leave circles blank if there are too many or add circles if there are not enough.

Draw a line from each circle to "ME" in the middle in the following way:

· Make the line thick (▬▬▬▬▬▬) for strong support and thin (──────────) for less strong support.

· Make the line solid (────────────) for more consistent support and broken (- - - - - - - - - - - - - - - - - -) for less frequent and less consistent support.

· Make the line straight (────────────) for helpful support and wavy (∧∧∧∧∧∧∧∧) for unhelpful or harmful support.

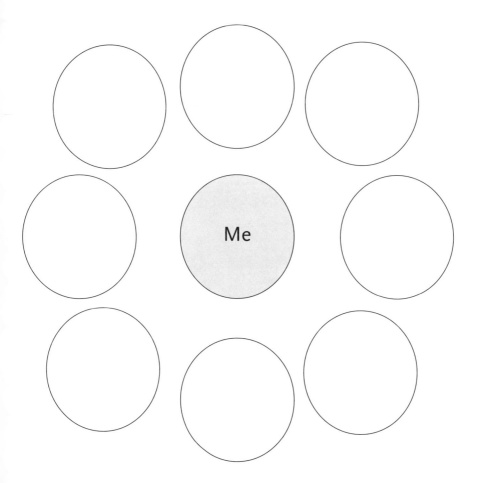

Recognizing and accessing support

Who has given me support?

_____

Who else might I turn to for support?

_____

_____

What professional or support resources have been helpful?

_____

_____

What other professional or support resources might be helpful?

_____

What gets in the way of accessing support from others?

_____

_____

How can I rely more on others for support?

_____

_____

What support will I access this week?

_____

How I felt before, during and after accessing this support:

Before: _____

During: _____

After: _____

Managing stress

OBJECTIVES

· to help group members identify what stressors they face and how they react to them
· to provide information on stress and ways of managing it
· to help group members understand methods of dealing with stress and to encourage them to work on one method

HANDOUTS

5-1: Stressor Checklist
5-2: Managing Stress
5-3: Practising Managing Stress

SESSION OUTLINE

· Opening and announcements (approx. 5 min.)
· Check-in and review of last week's home practice (approx. 30 min.)
· Teaching and discussion (approx. 60 min.)
· Assigning of next week's home practice (approx. 5 min.)
· Closing (approx. 5 min.)

Teaching and discussion

SOURCES OF STRESS

Ask the group members to define stressors (*stressors* are events or situations in our lives that we must cope with, or that we must adjust to). Explain that stressors are not necessarily events or situations that are viewed as negative. Funerals and marriages are both considered stressors, even though they are generally viewed respectively as negative and positive events. Also explain that stressors may be major life events (e.g., the birth of a child, the loss of a job), ongoing problems (e.g., poverty, health problems) or simply daily hassles (e.g., transportation difficulties, child care issues).

▶ **Distribute or turn to Handout 5-1: Stressor Checklist. Ask the participants to complete the handout.**

The purpose of the checklist is to help them to think of their own stressors. It is not meant to be an exhaustive list. Encourage them to write down any stressors (positive or negative) they are dealing with, if these are not included in the lists.

What stressors or difficulties are they facing, *apart from those related to their relative's substance use?*

▶ **Divide the blackboard, whiteboard or flipchart into two columns, and write the responses in the left column.**

Ask the group members what stressors or difficulties they are facing *as a result of the person's substance use.*

▶ **Write these responses in the right column.**

The main goal of this session is for group members to improve their ability to cope with stress in general, including the stress caused by familial substance use. By improving their ability to cope with any stress, participants will have greater resources to deal with the stress resulting from their relationship with someone who has a substance use problem.

Ask the group members to discuss how the stressors resulting from familial substance use interact with the other stressors in their life.

Explain that some exposure to stressors is considered healthy and can help us to grow, learn and function optimally. However, having many stressors typically results in our being unable to cope, having insufficient personal resources, feeling stressed, and having emotional and physical health problems.

MANAGING STRESS

Explain that we do not necessarily experience stressors as "stressful." We experience stress when we perceive that the demands of a situation exceed our resources.

Some people seem to experience more stressors than others. Acknowledge that people affected by familial substance use problems usually face multiple stressors. Validate the stress that group members feel given how many difficult stressors they have been dealing with, in some cases for a long time.

Ask the participants to talk about how they have been managing their stress. What personal or external resources have they been using that have helped them manage their stress?

▶ Write the responses on a blackboard, whiteboard or flipchart.

Explain that there are three main ways to reduce our stress. We can:
· reduce the stressors
· decrease our perception of stress
· increase our resources.

These approaches are outlined below. As you discuss them, provide examples and ask the group members for their own examples.

Reduce stressors

Changing the situation in some way can reduce stressors. For example:
· If someone has been stealing money from a participant, the participant can take steps to secure his or her finances (e.g., by locking up his or her wallet or by changing bank accounts or passwords).
· If a participant is experiencing physical health problems, he or she can seek medical treatment and take steps to deal with the medical problem.

Decrease the perception of stress

Changing how the situation or event is perceived can help reduce the perception of stress.

For example, if a participant believes that it is impossible to tolerate his or her current job, and it is not practical to change jobs, the person can think about what is positive about the job and what can be done to make it more tolerable (e.g., "My job provides me with an income, structure and the opportunity to learn English. I will try to get to know more colleagues as a way to make the job more tolerable. I am looking for another job and believe that I can handle this job for a few more months.").

Increase resources

Participants can increase resources either by replenishing them or by finding more internal or external resources. For example, they can:

· refresh themselves through rest, relaxation and recreation
· take care of their health (e.g., by eating well, sleeping, exercising and getting adequate medical care)
· access emotional support (e.g., someone to listen), practical support (e.g., child care) or material or financial support (e.g., money for health expenses)
· develop new skills (e.g., by learning how to deal with a child's temper tantrums in a better way).

Ask the group members to talk about how their strategies for coping with stress fit into each of the above categories. The table on the next page gives some examples for each category.

▶ **Distribute or turn to Handout 5-2: Managing Stress.**

Go over the decision tree in the handout. Ask a group member for an example of a stressor and use that example as you work through the handout. If you have time do this a second time, demonstrate the process for both a "yes" response and a "no" response.

CULTURE AND COMMUNITY: RESOURCE OR CHALLENGE?

Ask the participants to identify ways in which their culture or faith (e.g., cultural or religious beliefs and attitudes) has helped them, or can help them, to cope with familial substance use problems and other stressors. Have they sought support, advice or help from anyone within their cultural community? If they have, what was that like? If they have not, what prevented them from doing so?

Ask the participants to identify ways in which their culture makes coping with familial substance use problems and/or other stressors more difficult. Examples might include:

· strong prohibition against substance use
· stigma and exclusion of people with substance use problems (and their family members)
· belief in the importance of keeping family matters secret
· tendency to discourage the use of professional services.

Strategies for coping with stress

REDUCE STRESSORS	Problem solve
	Take steps toward change
	Set limits
	Reduce responsibilities
DECREASE THE PERCEPTION OF STRESS	Accept the situation
	Pray or meditate
	Let go of the situation
	Express yourself (e.g., write)
	Engage in positive self-talk
	Remember how you have coped in the past
	Deal with one stressor and one moment at a time
	Find humour or something positive in a challenging situation
INCREASE RESOURCES	Seek professional help
	Access community resources
	Seek emotional support
	Ask for financial assistance
	Ask for practical help (e.g., cleaning or child care)
	Spend time with people
	Distract yourself (e.g., watch a movie)
	Educate yourself
	Exercise
	Find joy in life
	Get a massage
	Express your emotions (e.g., allow yourself to cry or laugh)
	Eat properly
	Get enough rest and sleep

Tell the group members that different cultures often have different attitudes toward seeking help for personal or family problems. Ask if they have any examples to offer from their experience of their own culture.

EXTERNAL RESOURCES

Ask the group members what resources they have found helpful in dealing with their relative's substance use problem. What resources have they found helpful in dealing with other stressors?

If they have not used external resources, what has prevented them from doing so? Barriers may include:
· experiences (or expectations) of discrimination when accessing services
· fear that accessing services and admitting difficulties might influence their application for citizenship
· fear that accessing services might result in their being stigmatized by family or community members
· fear of being judged or blamed
· fear that their values will clash with those of service providers
· concern that service providers will not understand or relate to their experiences or difficulties
· belief that people should be able to handle things themselves
· language barriers
· transportation difficulties
· financial difficulties
· lack of time
· lack of services or resources in their community.

Finding community resources

Discuss using online directories (e.g., 211Toronto, 211Ontario) and networking (e.g., approaching neighbours; schools; or synagogues, mosques or churches) to find community resources.

▶ **Provide a list of relevant community and ethno-specific resources that might be appropriate for family members from a specific community.**

Home practice

▶ **Distribute or turn to Handout 5-3: Practising Managing Stress.**

Ask the participants to take five minutes before they leave to complete the relevant sections, and then to follow through with their plan during the week.

Stressor checklist

Check which of the following stressors you are experiencing *now* or have experienced *in the past year*:

FAMILIAL STRESSORS

☐ family member (includes partner or close friend) with a substance use problem
☐ family member with a mental health problem
☐ family member with a physical health problem
☐ family member with a gambling problem
☐ isolation from family member
☐ recent or upcoming separation from family member
☐ death of a family member
☐ family violence
☐ family conflict
☐ engagement or marriage
☐ children in the home
    ☐ birth of a child
    ☐ children under the age of five
    ☐ children with emotional, behavioural or social difficulties
    ☐ children with academic or learning difficulties
    ☐ children with a physical health problem
☐ involvement with child welfare authorities
☐ other: _____

INTERNAL STRESSORS

☐ pregnancy
☐ miscarriage or abortion
☐ substance use problems
☐ mental health problems
☐ physical health problems
☐ emotional problems (e.g., loneliness, grief, worry)
☐ dental problems
☐ chronic pain
☐ recent trauma or accident
☐ other: _____

EXTERNAL STRESSORS

- ☐ unemployment
- ☐ underemployment (working too few hours or having a job below your qualifications)
- ☐ overemployment (working more than one job or working more than 50 hours a week)
- ☐ poor or demanding working conditions
- ☐ new job or recent change in job
- ☐ pursuing an education
- ☐ preparation for an exam
- ☐ settlement to Canada
- ☐ recent or upcoming move
- ☐ homelessness
- ☐ poor housing conditions
- ☐ violent neighbourhood
- ☐ drug activity in neighbourhood
- ☐ exposure to violence
- ☐ encounter with police
- ☐ legal problems
- ☐ discrimination
- ☐ learning English
- ☐ poverty
- ☐ lack of health coverage
- ☐ other: _____

Managing stress

In deciding how to deal with a stressor, use the following as a guide:

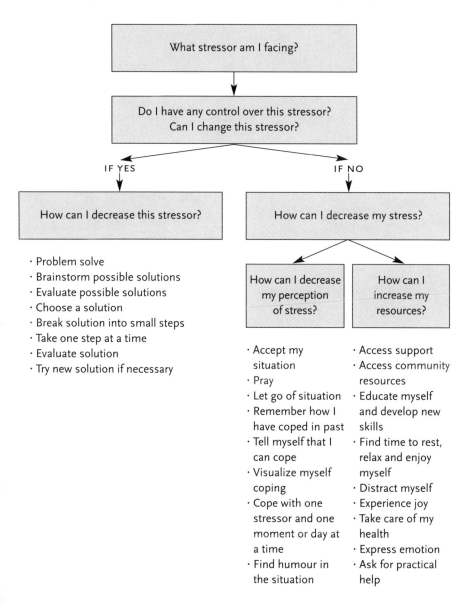

Practising managing stress

Identify and describe a stressor:_____

Ask whether you have control over the stressor and can change it.

If the answer is yes
Think about how you could decrease this stressor. Identify possible solutions and write them in the space below.

_____

_____

_____

Decide on one solution and write it in the space below.

_____

_____

Break down the solution into smaller steps:

1._____

_____

_____

2._____

_____

_____

3._____

_____

_____

4._____

_____

_____

Take the first step this week. Describe how you will reward yourself for taking this step.

_____

Evaluate your first step. How did it go?

_____

_____

If the answer is no

1. Determine how you can decrease your perception of stress. Write down one way that you will work on decreasing your perception of stress this week.

_____

_____

Describe the first step that you will you take to do this.

_____

_____

Evaluate this step. How did it go?

_____

_____

2. Determine how you can increase your resources. Write down one way in which you will increase your resources this week.

_____

_____

Describe the first step you will you take to do this.

_____

_____

Evaluate this first step. How did it go?

_____

_____

Using religious and spiritual resources

OBJECTIVES

· to help group members identify the role of spirituality, religion or faith in their lives and how it has been affected by substance use problems in the family
· to provide a comfortable environment and validation for group members who may have had negative experiences with religion or spirituality because of substance use problems in the family
· to enable group members to determine how their spirituality, religion or faith can help them deal with substance use problems in the family
· to encourage group members to share with one another examples of how their spirituality, religion or faith has helped them

HANDOUTS

6-1: My Religion, Spirituality or Faith

SESSION OUTLINE

· Opening and announcements (approx. 5 min.)
· Check-in and review of last week's home practice (approx. 30 min.)
· Teaching and discussion (approx. 60 min.)
· Assigning of next week's home practice (approx. 5 min.)
· Closing (approx. 5 min.)

CLIENT PREPARATION

At the previous session, ask the group members to identify a book, prayer, verse, saying, meditation, religious teaching, practice, service or religious leader that has been helpful or meaningful to them as they have coped with their relative's substance use problem. Request that they bring it, or information about it or a token representing it, to share with the group.

You may choose to invite a religious, spiritual or faith leader to this session. If so, you could ask the group members to come to the group with some questions for this leader.

Teaching and discussion

SPIRITUALITY, RELIGION AND FAITH AS A CHALLENGE AND/OR RESOURCE

Ask the group members how their spirituality, religion or faith has helped them deal with their situation.

Ask them to share what support their religious, spiritual or faith community offers and what support or help they have received. If they have asked for support or help, ask them to share their experiences of doing so and to evaluate if it was helpful. If they have not asked for support or help, ask what has prevented them from doing so.

Ask the group members to discuss teachings within their religion, spirituality or faith that relate to their family member's substance use (e.g., whether use of alcohol or other drugs is permitted). Also ask them how their religion, spirituality or faith affects the way in which they respond to their relative's substance use problems. For example, is separation or divorce permitted, and if so, under what conditions?

Ask the participants to talk about how their beliefs, practices or community have posed a challenge to them in dealing with a relative's substance use. How have they responded to these challenges? Have they experienced any conflicts between their own values and the values of service providers or treatment programs? If so, how have they have dealt with these value clashes? Examples might include the following:

· Their beliefs do not permit use of alcohol or other drugs, and yet the treatment program is based on harm reduction principles.
· They believe that divorce and separation are wrong, and yet they have been advised to leave their partner.

· They believe that family and community interdependency and self-sacrifice should be encouraged, but they have been encouraged to become more independent and self-serving.

Ask the participants how they and their relative are perceived (or would be perceived, should they disclose) by leaders and members of their religious, spiritual or faith community. Have they felt stigmatized because of the substance use problems? If so, how have they dealt with the stigma? Have they encountered people within their community who are more understanding and less judgmental?

FINDING MEANING

Ask the group members to consider what they have learned or how they have developed personally or spiritually as a result of their situation. For example, some people find that they:
· become closer to God
· find or develop their faith
· learn something new (e.g., about God, about life, about people, about themselves)
· become aware of how precious life is or particular relationships are
· learn who their supports and friends are
· develop a closer relationship with other family members
· learn about themselves, including their strengths and weaknesses
· strive for personal growth
· develop new priorities and goals
· become stronger
· become more compassionate and caring
· develop goals in terms of how they want to help others.

You may find it helpful to read a relevant quote that may prompt discussion. Below are two examples:

> In all of us there is a gift. Sometimes it is only in our darkness that we can finally see the light that shines from within.
> —Catherine Patterson-Sterling, *Rebuilding Relationships in Recovery: A Guide to Healing Relationships Impacted by Addiction*

It is in this whole process of meeting and solving problems that life has its meaning. Problems are the cutting edge that distinguishes between success and failure. Problems call forth our courage and our wisdom. It is only because of problems that we grow mentally and spiritually. . . . It is through the pain of confronting and resolving problems that we learn.

—M. Scott Peck, *The Road Less Traveled:
A New Psychology of Love*

HEARING FROM A RELIGIOUS, SPIRITUAL OR FAITH LEADER

If your group is predominantly from one faith community, you might choose to invite a leader from that community to speak to the group. If the group is mixed, you might want to invite more than one faith leader (or someone who is trained in and accustomed to working with people from different faith groups). You might ask these spiritual leaders to share appropriate insights with the group, or to answer questions that group members might have, to provide a list of faith-based resources, and to facilitate an appropriate spiritual exercise with the group.

SHARING

Ask the group members to share a resource that has been particularly helpful or meaningful to them in dealing with their relative's substance use (see "Client Preparation"). This could be a book, prayer, verse, saying, meditation, religious teaching, practice, service or religious leader.

Personal exercise and home practice

▶ **Distribute or turn to Handout 6-1: My Religion, Spirituality or Faith.**

Before the group members leave, ask them to complete the handout and then share with the group one thing that they plan to do in the following week with regard to their religion, spirituality or faith (e.g., talk to a spiritual leader, recite a prayer, attend a faith service). Encourage them to follow through with their plan.

References

Patterson-Sterling, C. (2004). *Rebuilding Relationships in Recovery: A Guide to Healing Relationships Impacted by Addiction.* Philadelphia, PA: Xlibris Corporation.

Peck, M.S. (1978). *The Road Less Traveled: A New Psychology of Love.* New York: Simon and Schuster.

My religion, spirituality or faith

How has your religion, spirituality or faith helped you in dealing with your relative's substance use problems?

_____

_____

_____

How can you better use your religion, spirituality or faith as a resource in dealing with your relative's substance use?

_____

_____

_____

What challenges have you faced in dealing with your relative's substance use, as a result of your religion, spirituality or faith?

_____

_____

_____

How can you improve the way you deal with these challenges?

_____

_____

_____

What step will you take this week to foster your religion, spirituality or faith?

_____

_____

_____

_____

Staying safe and managing crises

OBJECTIVES

· to normalize group members' experience in relation to managing crises and unsafe situations
· to validate group members' experiences of feeling out of control and unsafe
· to help group members learn ways to manage crises and stay safe

HANDOUTS

7-1: Tips for Managing Crises
7-2: Tips for Staying Safe
7-3: Planning for Crises
7-4: Planning for Safety

SESSION OUTLINE

· Opening and announcements (approx. 5 min.)
· Check-in and review of last week's home practice (approx. 30 min.)
· Teaching and discussion (approx. 60 min.)
· Assigning of next week's home practice (approx. 5 min.)
· Closing (approx. 5 min.)

Teaching and discussion

MANAGING CRISES

▶ Begin by saying that families affected by substance use problems often experience multiple problems and crises. Ask the group members to share crises that their family has recently experienced. Write the responses on a blackboard, whiteboard or flipchart.

Try dividing the examples they give into two categories:
· crises experienced by the person with a substance use problem
· crises experienced by other family members.

If you need more examples, you may choose some from the lists below.

Examples of crises experienced by the person with a substance use problem:
· serious medical problems due to the effects of substance use (e.g., seizures, overdoses)
· serious mental health problems (e.g. self-harming behaviour, psychotic episodes, severe depression, suicide attempts)
· serious legal problems (e.g., arrest warrant, criminal charge)
· serious behavioural problems (e.g., violence, stealing, drug dealing, drunk driving)
· serious problems of living (e.g., loss of housing, loss of job, loss of children, indebtedness)
· serious relational problems (e.g., interpersonal violence, threats of violence from drug dealers).

Examples of crises experienced by other family members:
· serious medical problems related to stress (e.g., heart attack, eating disorder)
· serious mental health problems (e.g., depression, acute anxiety, suicide attempts)
· serious legal problems
· safety concerns related to the behaviour of the person with a substance use problem (e.g., threats of violence, stolen or destroyed property)
· financial problems
· involvement of child welfare authorities.

Explain that we cannot prevent all crises, but we can prevent ourselves from living in "crisis mode." Ask the group members what it is like to live in crisis mode, and what the repercussions of this way of living are for them and their families. Ask how they believe they might be able to prevent this mode of living.

Explain that two ways to decrease the likelihood of living in crisis mode are:
· dealing with small problems as they arise
· planning ahead for how they will handle crises.

Ask a group member who has recently experienced a crisis and believes that he or she handled it well to share the details of the crisis and his or her response. If no one volunteers, ask someone who has recently experienced a crisis and does *not* believe that he or she handled it well to share the details instead. The group can then discuss what that person could have done differently.

Ask the participants for tips on managing crises.

▶ **Then distribute or turn to Handout 7-1: Tips for Managing Crises.**

Go over each tip together. Explain the importance of having a plan and being willing to follow through with it. (For example, most people have difficulty calling for emergency services to deal with a crisis involving a family member with a substance use problem. Discuss what prevents them from doing so.)

As you work through the handout, use one or more of the following examples or one that you believe is relevant:
· Your mother is trying to stop drinking alcohol. You hear a noise and run upstairs to discover that she is having a seizure.
· Drug dealers arrive at the door demanding to see your son. They claim that he owes them money and that they will kill him if he does not pay.
· Your sister calls saying how depressed she is about her substance use and what a bad mother she has been to her children. She says she feels hopeless and would like to die, and that her children would be better off without her. She plans to take a bottle of Tylenol that evening.
· Your partner comes home from a bar and begins slamming doors, yelling and throwing objects. He is angry that you have not yet put the children to bed and accuses you of being a bad mother.
· You call your daughter, who is at her father's home for a visit. He answers and you realize that he is drunk, but he denies it. When you tell him that you are coming to get your daughter, he insists that he is taking her to the zoo as planned and that you can't stop him.
· Your son calls to say that he has lost his job and has not been making the payments on his apartment, and so is at risk of being evicted.

STAYING SAFE

One type of crisis involves a threat to the family's safety. Group members may be concerned about their emotional, physical, sexual or financial safety and security. Discuss the link between substance use and safety issues (e.g., the associations between alcohol and violence, and between cocaine use and stealing).

Ask if the group members have felt unsafe within their relationship with the person who has a substance use problem. Point out that their lack of safety may relate to fears both of what their relative might do, or of what they might do themselves.

Ask the group members in what way have they felt unsafe (e.g., emotionally, physically). What made them feel unsafe (e.g., behaviour or statements from the other person or from themselves, or particular situations)? Emphasize that there is no right or wrong answer and that everyone reacts to situations differently. What makes one person feel unsafe may not make someone else feel unsafe.

▶ **Make a list of these behaviours, statements and situations on a blackboard, whiteboard or flipchart.**

Ask the group members to discuss what they have done to keep themselves safe. Brainstorm other ways to ensure their own safety and the safety of their family.

▶ **Distribute or turn to Handout 7-2: Tips for Staying Safe.**

Go over each point together. Explain that if anyone has concerns about his or her own physical, emotional or sexual safety, or the safety of another family member, the person can speak to one of the facilitators after the session; the facilitator will then schedule an appointment to help the person develop a safety plan.

Home practice

▶ **Distribute or turn to Handout 7-3: Planning for Crises, and Handout 7-4: Planning for Safety.**

Ask the group members to complete these handouts during the week.

For more information

For more information on helping family members stay safe, please refer to the following book:

Meyers, R.J. & Wolfe, B.L. (2004). *Get Your Loved One Sober: Alternatives to Nagging, Pleading, and Threatening.* Center City, MN : Hazelden Press.

Tips for managing crises

BE CALM

Be prepared

Exercise caution

Calm down

Assess the situation

Lessen the intensity of the situation

Model confidence and control

Be prepared

Try to foresee possible crises, and plan what you will do if a crisis occurs. If possible, involve the person with a substance use problem, as well as treatment providers, in developing a plan. Have a list of emergency phone numbers, including those of a doctor, a treatment provider, a hospital emergency department and the police. The list should also include the numbers of child care providers, family members or supportive friends.

Exercise caution

Be careful. If there is a risk of harm, avoid any action that will make the situation worse; remove yourself or others from the situation; and/or call for help (this includes calling the police or calling for an ambulance, if necessary).

Calm down

Control your emotions. Try to avoid intense feelings of anger or anxiety. Focus on your breathing. If necessary, remove yourself from the situation until you are more under control.

Assess the situation

Try to take the situation seriously without "catastrophizing" (automatically assuming the worst). Decide what plan will best allow you to deal with the situation. If you already have a plan, decide if it will work in this situation.

Lessen the intensity of the situation

Speak quietly. Slow down your breathing, thoughts and actions. Reduce distractions. Validate people's emotions (i.e., let them know that it's OK to feel how they feel and that their feelings make sense).

Model confidence and control

Act and speak with confidence and assertiveness. Take control of the situation and of your behaviour.

Tips for staying safe

BE SAFE

Be prepared

Exercise caution

Spot danger signs

Assess the situation

Figure out a solution

Enforce limits

Be prepared

Try to foresee situations in which you or someone else may become unsafe, and plan what you will do if this occurs. Have a list of emergency phone numbers, including those of a doctor, a treatment provider, a hospital emergency department, a child welfare agency (in Ontario, a Children's Aid Society), the police, child care providers, and family members or supportive friends. Have a getaway bag (including, for example, phone numbers, money, keys and clothing) hidden but easily accessible so you can take it with you in an emergency.

Exercise caution

If there is a risk of harm, do not take any action that will make the situation worse. Remove yourself or others from the situation and/or call for help (including calling for the police or for an ambulance). Try to control your emotions. Do not judge, argue, provoke, patronize, mock or invalidate (i.e., tell the person that his or her feelings are wrong or don't make sense) the person. Remember, your safety is more important than winning an argument.

Spot danger signs

Pay attention to any signs of increasing violence. Notice looks (e.g., glares), words (e.g., swearing, accusations, threats), behaviours (e.g., slamming doors) or other signs (e.g., several empty beer bottles) that someone may be unsafe.

Assess the situation

Assess the risk to your own safety and that of others. Recall previous situations, including what the person with a substance use problem has done in the past and what happened as a result. (Past behaviour is often a good predictor of current or future behaviour.) Respect your gut feeling about the seriousness of the situation.

Figure out a solution

Act quickly yet thoughtfully. Decide what plan would be best to use in dealing with the situation. If you already have a plan, decide if it will work in this situation.

Enforce limits

Stay firm in the limits you have set with regard to safety issues. If the person with a substance use problem does not respect those limits, enforce them by doing what you have said you will do (even if this might mean calling the police or reporting violence).

Planning for crises

What is a possible crisis that you might encounter?

_____

_____

What safety concerns might arise for you or others during this crisis?

_____

_____

Use the following as a guide to help you plan for how you will handle the situation:

Be prepared:_____

_____

Exercise caution: _____

_____

Calm down: _____

_____

Assess the situation:_____

_____

Lessen the intensity of the situation:_____

_____

Model confidence and control: _____

_____

Planning for safety

What is a possible unsafe situation that you might encounter?

_____

_____

What about the situation makes you feel unsafe?

_____

_____

What warning signs indicate that things are becoming unsafe?

_____

_____

Use the following as a guide to help you plan for how you will handle the situation:

Be prepared:_____

_____

Exercise caution: _____

_____

Spot danger signs: _____

_____

Assess the situation: _____

_____

Figure out a solution:_____

_____

Enforce limits:_____

_____

Grieving and coping

OBJECTIVES

· to help group members identify what they have lost because of their relative's substance use
· to validate group members' experiences of loss
· to help group members become aware of how they have been grieving their losses
· to encourage group members to allow themselves to grieve

HANDOUTS

8-1: Acknowledging Losses
8-2: Understanding and Managing Grief
8-3: Grieving and Coping with Losses

SESSION OUTLINE

· Opening and announcements (approx. 5 min.)
· Check-in and review of last week's home practice (approx. 30 min.)
· Teaching and discussion (approx. 60 min.)
· Assigning of next week's home practice (approx. 5 min.)
· Closing (approx. 5 min.)

Teaching and discussion

LOSSES DUE TO SUBSTANCE USE

The losses associated with a person's problematic substance use are far-reaching. They extend beyond the person himself or herself to the person's partner, parents, children, siblings, other relatives, friends, colleagues, neighbours and others.

Ask the group members to identify the losses experienced by the person in their family with a substance use problem.

▶ **Write down the answers on a blackboard, whiteboard or flipchart.**

Then distribute or turn to Handout 8-1: Acknowledging Losses.

Ask the participants to spend about five minutes listing losses that they themselves have experienced because of their relative's substance use. Encourage them to share examples from their list.

▶ **Write the responses in a separate column or on a separate piece of chart paper.**

Reactions to loss

Ask the group members how they have reacted to the losses. Validate their attempts to deal with a difficult situation. Keep this discussion brief, because later you will ask them for more details about grieving and coping responses.

▶ **Distribute or turn to Handout 8-2: Understanding and Managing Grief.**

Describe the stages of grief. Ask the group members to identify which stages they have been in with regard to their relative's substance use, and which stage they are currently in.

Discuss why grieving the losses associated with a family member's substance use is more complicated than grieving a death (see Handout 8-2). For example, death is final, occurs to everyone and (in most cases) is not stigmatized. In addition, society permits people time to grieve deaths and provides appropriate avenues and rituals through which to grieve, as well as providing support to the bereaved.

▶ **Distribute or turn to Handout 8-3: Grieving and Coping with Losses. Ask the participants to complete questions 1, 2, 3 and 6.**

Then encourage them to share how they have grieved, and to brainstorm other possible ways of grieving.

Do not criticize the ways in which the group members have tried coping, although you may want to highlight the healthier ways of coping that they have identified. You may also want to ask the participants what the consequences of their methods of coping were.

Emphasize that during the group you will frequently discuss healthy ways of coping, so that participants can add to their repertoire of coping methods.

Home practice

Ask the group members to complete the remaining parts of Handout 8-3. In doing so, they will choose and try out new ways to help them grieve and to cope. At the next session, they will report back to the group on how their strategies worked.

Acknowledging losses

What have you lost because of your family member's substance use?

_____

_____

_____

_____

_____

_____

_____

_____

_____

_____

_____

_____

Understanding and managing grief

STAGES OF GRIEF

Grief is a natural and necessary reaction to loss. Here are some stages of grief[1] that people often experience, and typical statements that people in each stage may make. (These stages are not necessarily experienced one after the other, separately or in this order.)

SHOCK AND DISBELIEF

"My child must be going through a phase."
"I can't have married someone and not known that she had a problem with alcohol."

BARGAINING

"Everything will be OK if I can just get her into treatment."
"I will do whatever you [e.g., God, or the person with a substance use problem] want if you will just make things better."
"I will work harder at being supportive so things will improve."

ANGER

"Why is this happening to me?"
"She has wrecked my life."
"I hate him for what he has done to me and my family."

SADNESS

"I am overwhelmed with sadness about my relationship."
"I feel so depressed. I don't know if I will ever be happy again."
"I am so disappointed for my child. He had such potential and is throwing that away."

ACCEPTANCE

"This is not what I had hoped for in a partnership. I will try to figure out how I will cope and continue with my life."
"I recognize that my child has a substance use problem and feel very sad about it. I need to take care of myself and figure out the best way to support him."

---

1. Adapted from Kübler Ross, E. (1997). *On Death and Dying*. New York: Touchstone.

GRIEVING THE LOSSES ASSOCIATED WITH SUBSTANCE USE

Grieving because of a relative's substance use is often difficult because:

· you may not experience closure, because the problem may be ongoing
· you may keep your grief private, feeling unable to share the experience with others because of possible shame and stigma
· you often must carry on with your own and sometimes your relative's responsibilities, and so have little time to reflect and grieve
· society does not recognize and validate these losses and has no common rituals that you can use to cope with your grief.

DEALING WITH GRIEF

Here are some ways to help you deal with your grief:

· Acknowledge what you have lost.
· Validate and accept the grieving process.
· Share your grief with others.
· Develop rituals to help you deal with your grief.

Grieving and coping with losses

1. Circle the stages of grief that you have been in:

Shock and disbelief   Bargaining   Anger   Sadness   Acceptance

2. Circle the stage(s) of grief that you are in now:

Shock and disbelief   Bargaining   Anger   Sadness   Acceptance

3. What have you done to allow yourself to grieve the losses?

_____

_____

4. What is one way that you can help yourself to grieve this week?

_____

_____

5. What did you do and how did it go?

_____

_____

6. How have you coped with the losses?

_____

_____

7. What is one healthy way that you can help yourself to cope this week?

_____

_____

8. What did you do and how did it go?

_____

_____

Managing emotions

OBJECTIVES

· to help group members identify what emotions they are experiencing
· to validate group members' emotional reactions to their situation
· to provide information about emotions and how to manage them
· to encourage group members to become aware of how they are managing
  their emotions and how (or whether) these methods are effective
· to help group members improve on or develop new methods of managing
  difficult emotions

HANDOUTS

9-1: Understanding Our Emotions
9-2: Managing Emotions
9-3: Managing Difficult Emotions
9-4: Practising Managing Emotions
9-5: Managing Anxiety
9-6: Practising Managing Anxiety
9-7: Cognitive-Behavioural Techniques for Managing Anxiety
9-8: Managing Sadness and Depression
9-9: Practising Managing Sadness and Depression
9-10: Cognitive-Behavioural Techniques for Managing Depression
9-11: Managing Guilt and Shame
9-12: Determining Responsibility
9-13: Practising Managing Guilt and Shame
9-14: Managing Anger
9-15: Cognitive-Behavioural Techniques for Managing Anger
9-16: Practising Managing Anger
9-17: Books for Managing Emotions

SESSION OUTLINE

· Opening and announcements (approx. 5 min.)
· Check-in and review of last week's home practice (approx. 30 min.)
· Teaching and discussion (approx. 60 min.)
· Assigning of next week's home practice (approx. 5 min.)
· Closing (approx. 5 min.)

CLIENT PREPARATION

At the previous session, distribute Handout 9-1: Understanding Our Emotions. If that was not possible and group members have access to e-mail, send it to them electronically. Ask that they read it prior to the session.

NOTE: We recommend that you take more than one session to complete this module, beginning with Part 1: Understanding and Managing Emotions, and then choosing one or more emotions to work on in greater detail in Part 2: Managing Specific Emotions. If you can only do one session on emotions, we recommend that you do Part 1.

HANDOUTS FOR PART 1

9-1: Understanding Our Emotions
9-2: Managing Emotions
9-3: Managing Difficult Emotions
9-4: Practising Managing Emotions
9-17: Books for Managing Emotions

HANDOUTS FOR PART 2

One or more of:
9-5: Managing Anxiety
9-8: Managing Sadness and Depression
9-11: Managing Guilt and Shame
9-14: Managing Anger
One or more of:
9-7: Cognitive-Behavioural Techniques for Managing Anxiety
9-10: Cognitive-Behavioural Techniques for Managing Depression
9-12: Determining Responsibility
9-15: Cognitive-Behavioural Techniques for Managing Anger
One or more of:
9-6: Practising Managing Anxiety
9-9: Practising Managing Sadness and Depression
9-13: Practising Managing Guilt and Shame
9-16: Practising Managing Anger

Part 1: Understanding and managing emotions

TEACHING AND DISCUSSION

Ask the group members to name feelings they have experienced within the context of their family member's substance use.

▶ **Write the responses on a blackboard, whiteboard or flipchart.**

Validate and normalize these emotional reactions.

▶ **Distribute or turn to Handout 9-1: Understanding our Emotions.**

The group members were asked at the previous session to read this handout at home, but if many of them have not done so, you may decide to read it together as a group. Ask each group member to comment on one of the points that he or she found particularly interesting, enlightening or helpful, or found confusing.

If necessary, use the points below to aid discussing the points in more detail. It is important that the group members have some understanding of emotions, but we advise that you spend more time on how to manage emotions.

Discussion points: Understanding our emotions

EMOTIONS SHOULD BE ACCEPTED

The first step in managing emotions is acknowledging their presence and accepting them. Emotions are a natural human phenomenon. We are more able to manage our emotions when we validate and accept them, rather than fighting, denying or chronically suppressing them. (Sometimes, though, we may mindfully choose to temporarily suppress emotions, with the intention of processing and managing these emotions at a more appropriate time.)

Ask the group members what happens when they fight or deny their emotions. Use an analogy to explain the importance of accepting emotions. For example:

· Chronically suppressed sadness is like a weed in a garden that is ignored, allowing it to spread throughout the garden and prevent the growth of more desirable plants.
· Chronically suppressed anger is like a cancer that if undetected, ignored, denied or untreated, grows and infects the entire body and becomes unmanageable.

EMOTIONS MAY BE HIDDEN

Emotions may be hidden and yet may still affect our behaviour. We are able to manage our emotions better when we recognize them. We can often identify what we are feeling by pausing and paying attention to (being mindful of) our bodies, emotions and thoughts.

Ask the group members to state how they know that they are feeling a certain emotion. What are the physiological and cognitive indicators of our primary emotions?

EMOTIONS VARY IN INTENSITY

Emotions often increase in intensity gradually. We are more able to deal with emotions at low intensities, so it is helpful to pay continual attention to (be mindful of) our bodies, emotions and thoughts, and to deal with emotions as soon as we become aware of them.

Ask the group members if they ever suddenly feel intensely angry without having noticed becoming so. Ask them to spend one minute being mindful of their bodies, thoughts and feelings. Encourage them to pause periodically to check what they are feeling.

EMOTIONS SERVE A PURPOSE

One purpose of emotions is to convey to ourselves and others how we are doing and what might need to be changed.

Ask the group members to think about a recent emotion they had and to consider what purpose it served. You may wish to give a made-up example. For instance, you might say:

> I was so angry when I came home from work and found my wife passed out on the floor and my young children messy, hungry, upset and unsupervised. This anger made me aware of how intolerable this situation was to me and to our children, and that it could not continue. The next day, I communicated my anger to my wife and informed her that she could no longer be trusted to care for the children.

EMOTIONS MAY NOT OCCUR ALONE

We may feel multiple emotions when dealing with complex situations. Most group members will relate to this experience. You might want to ask them for a few examples.

EMOTIONS MAY BE PRIMARY OR SECONDARY

Secondary emotions often mask underlying primary emotions and complicate how we understand and manage our feelings. For instance:

· anger can mask feeling hurt or disappointed
· anxiety can mask feeling sad or depressed
· shame can mask feeling anxious or worried
· anger can mask feeling angry at someone else.

Emphasize the importance of acknowledging, dealing with and communicating the primary emotion. We need to determine what our primary emotion is so that we can actually deal with this emotion.

EMOTIONS MAY BE AFFECTED BY OUR BEING PHYSICALLY VULNERABLE

Emotions may be more difficult to deal with and seem more intense when we are physically vulnerable. Emphasize the need for group members to take care of themselves by getting adequate health care, sleep, food and exercise. They also need to manage or reduce their own substance use, because substances usually increase our vulnerability to emotions and prevent us from dealing with emotions effectively.

Most people will agree that it is important to take care of oneself. Nonetheless, it is still important to emphasize this point and to encourage participants to try to prevent themselves from becoming vulnerable, or to be aware of when they feel vulnerable. You may also wish to discuss the influence of fluctuating hormone levels (e.g., during menstruation, pregnancy, menopause) on emotional vulnerability. Ask the group members what they think they could do to decrease their physical vulnerability.

EMOTIONS MAY BE EXHAUSTING AND OVERWHELMING

We can take breaks from dealing with difficult emotions by temporarily distracting ourselves. For example, we can exercise, watch a movie, take a shower or read a book.

Although we do not recommend that group members always distract themselves from their emotions, temporary distraction can help prevent them from becoming overwhelmed by their emotions and possibly behaving in a way that they would later regret. You may encourage participants to give themselves permission to deal with emotions in small, manageable chunks.

EMOTIONS CAN BE TOLERATED AND MANAGED

Emotions come and go and change in intensity over time. We can ride emotional experiences like a surfer rides waves. We can remind ourselves while experiencing emotions that the feeling will pass. We might be able to help ourselves tolerate difficult emotions by engaging in soothing activities (e.g., taking a bath, going for a walk, sipping herbal tea, listening to music).

Knowing that we can tolerate and manage emotions is particularly important when we are experiencing intensely painful or frightening emotions. People can tolerate intense emotions and will notice that their feelings gradually decrease in intensity. You may want to tell the group members that when they become more aware of their emotions they will discover that emotional intensity continually fluctuates. When people look back at their emotional experience, they rarely see the fluctuations, but when they become mindful of their emotions in the moment, they notice the changes in intensity.

EMOTIONS ARE MORE EASILY ADDRESSED WITH THE SUPPORT OF TRUSTED OTHERS

We can better deal with our emotions when we experience the validation and comfort of friends, family members or professionals. We do not have to manage alone.

You may wish to ask the participants what it has been like to share their emotions with the facilitators and/or the group.

There is great comfort in being heard, validated and supported by another person. Praise participants for having shared their emotions with the facilitators and the group.

EMOTIONS CAN BE REDUCED OR CHANGED

Emotions are valid, yet we may want to reduce their intensity or change them because:

· they may interfere with our health (e.g., we feel so anxious that we are chronically experiencing physiological symptoms)
· they may impede appropriate action (e.g., we feel so much rage that we cannot think clearly enough to devise a plan to improve the situation)
· they may be too intense and overwhelming (e.g., we feel so sad that we feel helpless and hopeless about our situation)
· they may not be warranted by a situation (e.g., we might feel ashamed of our family member's substance use).

People can sometimes feel invalidated when someone suggests that they reduce the intensity of an emotion or change it. Given this, we recommend that you develop some personalized examples of when group members might want to modify their emotions.

EMOTIONS ARE INTERCONNECTED WITH OUR THOUGHTS AND BEHAVIOURS

Emotions are influenced by our thoughts, so we can change our emotions by changing our thoughts.

Likewise, emotions are influenced by our behaviour, so we can change our emotions by changing our behaviour. We can often succeed at changing our emotion if we act the opposite way to how we feel.

Ask the group members for examples of how their thoughts, feelings and behaviour interconnect. You may also give your own examples.

▶ **On a blackboard, whiteboard or flipchart, you may wish to draw a diagram of a triangle to show the relationships among thoughts, feelings and behaviours. Outside of the triangle, show that all three are influenced by the environment.**

You may also wish to use an example such as the following to illustrate how our thoughts influence our emotions:

> I walked outside and noticed how cold it was. I thought to myself that this winter was the worst I had ever experienced and would be the death of me. I felt defeated and depressed.

> I walked outside and noticed how cold it was. I thought to myself how crisp the air felt and how much it made me aware of being alive. I felt energetic and joyful.

You may wish to use a similar example to illustrate how our behaviour influences our emotions:

> I felt down and discouraged. After my kids left for school, I went back to bed. When it was time for me to pick up my kids from school, I felt worse and didn't know how I was going to get myself out of bed. I called my husband and asked that he pick them up. I felt lethargic, hopeless and a failure.

> I felt down and discouraged. After my kids went to school, I felt like going back to bed, but instead I got dressed and ate breakfast. Then I went for a walk in the local park on my way to the grocery store. I came home and cleaned the bathroom and did some gardening. Then I called my friend to meet me for tea before picking up the kids from school. As the day went on, my

mood improved. I was still somewhat down and less energetic than usual, but I was managing. I was excited to see my kids.

EMOTIONS MAY INDICATE A NEED FOR PROFESSIONAL ASSISTANCE

We may need to seek mental health treatment for problems with anxiety, depression, shame or anger.

Suggest to participants that if they are having considerable difficulty with these emotions, they can speak to you after the group and you might be able to help them find appropriate services.

Managing emotions

▶ **Distribute or turn to Handout 9-3: Managing Difficult Emotions. Ask the participants to complete the first three questions and to share their responses with the group.**

▶ **Write down the strategies used by the participants on a blackboard, whiteboard or flipchart.**

Reinforce effective emotion management strategies and efforts to try different strategies.

▶ **Distribute or turn to Handout 9-2: Managing Emotions.**

Read and discuss the strategies that are outlined for managing emotions.

▶ **Turn again to Handout 9-3. Instruct the group members to mark which strategies they have been using successfully in managing their emotions.**

Now distribute or turn to Handout 9-4: Practising Managing Emotions.

Ask the group members to complete the first two questions and to report to the group what they will be working on during the week. Encourage them to try a new strategy for managing a difficult emotion.

HOME PRACTICE

Ask the group members to work on managing an emotion in a different way in at least one situation and to record how it went on Handout 9-4.

▶ **Distribute or turn to Handout 9-17: Books for Managing Emotions.**

Part 2: Managing specific emotions

TEACHING AND DISCUSSION

Decide which emotion(s) you will discuss during the group. You may solicit input from the group members on what emotions they wish to focus on during this session. We advise that you cover one emotion (or at most two) thoroughly and, if you wish to discuss another emotion, that you take an additional week to do so.

▶ **Distribute or turn to the appropriate handout:**

9-5: Managing Anxiety (see discussion points below)
9-8: Managing Sadness and Depression (see discussion points on page 167)
9-11: Managing Guilt and Shame (see discussion points on page 173)
9-14: Managing Anger (see discussion points on page 179).

Anxiety

UNDERSTANDING ANXIETY

▶ **Make three columns on a blackboard, whiteboard or flipchart. In the first column write the heading "Situations," in the second column write "Thoughts" and in the third column write "Responses."**

Ask the group members to share when they feel afraid, anxious or nervous in relation to their family member's problematic substance use, and what it is that causes them to have these feelings. Write their responses in the first column. Ask them then to identify what they worry about in relation to the substance use, and write the responses in the second column. Finally, ask them to report what they experience physiologically and what they do behaviourally when they feel anxious, and fill in the third column.

Comment on the different components of anxiety and how they relate to each other: the environment, thoughts, physiology and behaviour. Emphasize the role of thoughts in anxiety. You might also want to explain that when people feel anxious, they tend to experience the following:
· an obsession with "what if" thoughts (e.g., they might ask, "What if I fail?" "What if he drinks?" "What if someone judges me?")
· a tendency to over-predict the possibility of negative outcomes
· a tendency to underestimate their ability to handle life in general, stress and even negative outcomes

· an intolerance of uncertainty (e.g., they want to know and figure out everything in advance, and agonize about making the right decision)
· a tendency to engage in cognitive errors (e.g., catastrophizing, all-or-nothing thinking, personalization).

Explain that often, fear is a natural and healthy response to a potentially dangerous situation. The anxiety serves a purpose, communicating that something is wrong and must be changed. Anxiety may indicate that someone is not safe. Ask the group members to look at the chart created earlier and to notice which situations indicate that someone is not safe. Recommend that group members pay attention to their anxiety, noticing if someone is unsafe and acting to reinstate safety if they can.

Here are some examples of occasions when group members might experience anxiety, and what they can do to ensure safety:
· Parents are worried that their son, who has a substance use problem, might drive under the influence of drugs. They decide to refuse him access to the family car.
· A woman is concerned that her children might not be safe because her ex-partner sometimes uses substances while visiting with the children and passes out. She decides to contact the Children's Aid Society, and together they determine that the visits must be supervised.
· A man fears his partner's angry words and rough behaviour when he drinks. He decides that whenever his partner drinks, he will leave their home and stay with a friend. He packs a "getaway bag" that he leaves close to the front door for quick exits.

Explain that, despite frequently being an appropriate reaction, the emotion of anxiety is at times unnecessary and interferes with daily life. In these cases, there is no threat to anyone's safety, just a *perceived* threat. For example, someone may fear speaking to a neighbour because of her concern that the neighbour may have seen her husband come home drunk and heard his yelling. She may worry that the neighbour will reject her and judge her for her husband's behaviour. This is possible, but energy spent avoiding the neighbour or fearing bumping into her might be a waste. It is just as possible that, if the family member gets up the courage to speak to the neighbour, she may discover that the neighbour is courteous and supportive.

Explain that, at other times, the emotion of anxiety does communicate that someone is unsafe, but there is nothing that can be done by the family member to increase safety. For example, the person may be fearful because the actions of the relative with a substance use problem are making him vulnerable (e.g., in danger of getting beaten up, getting into an accident or losing his job). Nonetheless, the family member may have little power to increase his or her relative's safety, and to do so might involve rescuing the relative (thus preventing the relative from experiencing the consequences of his or her use). In such cases, family members may need to let go of their feelings of responsibility, accept what they cannot change, and consider ways to reduce their worrying and anxiety.

Discuss how participants can recognize when their anxiety is not helpful and when they may need to talk to a health care professional. This decision is very subjective, but the following list may help guide group members in determining when they might seek professional help:

· when anxiety interferes with your daily functioning (e.g., going to work, looking after children, driving, attending appointments)
· when anxiety is distressing to you
· when anxiety is severe or chronic
· when anxiety negatively affects your health
· when you want to experience less anxiety and don't know how to do it on your · own, or have not been able to do it on your own.

MANAGING ANXIETY

▶ **Distribute or turn to Handout 9-5: Managing Anxiety. Ask the group members to complete the question at the top of the handout.**

Now turn to Handout 9-2: Managing Emotions.

Discuss with group members how these strategies, introduced in the previous session, would be relevant to managing anxiety.

▶ **When discussing how to reduce emotions, distribute or turn to Handout 9-7: Cognitive-Behavioural Techniques for Managing Anxiety.**

Instruct group members on some of these strategies. Select one behavioural technique and one cognitive technique to demonstrate and practise during the session.

▶ **Distribute or turn to Handout 9-6: Practising Managing Anxiety. Ask the participants to check off which approaches to managing their anxiety they want to work on in the upcoming week, and to note how they will put each approach into practice.**

HOME PRACTICE

Ask the group members to complete Handout 9-6 by practising new methods of managing anxiety and recording how it went. Ask that they read over Handout 9-2 and Handout 9-7 at home to remind them of effective methods of managing their anxiety.

FOR MORE INFORMATION

For more information on managing anxiety, see the following books:

Beck, A., Rush, J.A., Shaw, B.F. & Emery, G. (1987). *Cognitive Therapy of Depression*. New York: Guilford Press.

Beck, J. (1995). *Cognitive Therapy: Basics and Beyond*. New York: Guilford Press.

Davis, M., Robbins-Eshelman, E. & McKay, M. (2000). *The Relaxation and Stress Reduction Workbook* (5th ed.). Oakland, CA: New Harbinger Publications.

Greenberger, D. & Padesky, C.A. (1995). *Mind Over Mood: Change How You Feel by Changing the Way You Think*. New York: Guilford Press.

Linehan, M. (1993). *Cognitive-Behavioural Therapy of Borderline Personality Disorder*. New York: Guilford Press.

Sadness and depression

UNDERSTANDING SADNESS AND DEPRESSION

▶ **Make three columns on a blackboard, whiteboard or flipchart. In the first column write the heading "Situations," in the second column write "Thoughts" and in the third column write "Responses."**

Ask the group members to share when they feel down, sad, discouraged or depressed in relation to their family member's problematic substance use, and what it is that causes them to have these feelings. Write their responses in the first column. Ask them then to identify what they think about in relation to the substance use when they are feeling sad, and write the responses in the second column. Finally, ask them to report what they experience physiologically and what they do behaviourally when they feel sad, and fill in the third column.

Comment on the different components of sadness and depression and how they relate to each other: the environment, thoughts, physiology and behaviour. Emphasize the role of thoughts in sadness and depression. You might want to ask the group members to examine any patterns they see in the thoughts listed in the second column. People who feel sad typically think about what they or others have lost, and how they or others have been hurt. People who feel depressed tend to think negatively about the world (e.g., "No one cares about me," "No one can help us," "People are selfish"), themselves (e.g., "I'm no good," "I'm a failure") and the future (e.g., "I can't change," "Things will never get better"). They tend to focus on and remember only negative experiences and situations that confirm this negative thinking about the world, themselves and the future.

Validate group members' feelings of sadness. Explain that sadness and grief are normal and healthy responses to familial substance use. Emphasize that it is OK to feel sad or to grieve in such a situation. (For more information on grieving, see Module 8: Grieving and Coping.)

Discuss the difference between sadness and depression. Explain that depression is typically a feeling of sadness, emptiness and/or irritability that occurs most of the time and is accompanied by many other changes that interfere with regular functioning. These changes include:

· decreased interest and pleasure in most activities
· significant weight loss or gain
· difficulties sleeping, or oversleeping
· increased or decreased physical activity
· fatigue or loss of energy
· feelings of worthlessness or of guilt that is excessive or inappropriate
· decreased ability to think, concentrate or make decisions
· recurrent thoughts of death or killing oneself.

For more information on the criteria for diagnosing depression, see the DSM-IV (American Psychiatric Association, 1994).

Although depression may be an understood reaction to familial substance use problems, it is not healthy and should not be ignored. If a group member is experiencing depression, he or she should seek professional services.

Discuss how participants can recognize when their sadness and grieving is excessive and unhealthy. In addition to considering the symptoms listed above, group members may use the following guide to help them determine when they might seek professional help:

· When depression interferes with your daily functioning (e.g., going to work, looking after children, driving the car, attending appointments, etc).
· when depression is distressing to you
· when depression is severe or chronic
· when depression negatively affects your health
· when you want to feel less depressed and don't know how to achieve it on your own, or have not been able to do it on your own.

MANAGING SADNESS AND DEPRESSION

▶ **Distribute or turn to Handout 9-8: Managing Sadness and Depression. Ask the group members to complete the question at the top of the handout.**

Now turn to Handout 9-2: Managing Emotions.

Discuss with group members how these strategies, introduced in the previous session, would be relevant to managing sadness and depression.

▶ **When discussing how to reduce emotions, distribute or turn to Handout 9-10: Cognitive-Behavioural Techniques for Managing Depression.**

Instruct group members on some of these strategies. Select one behavioural technique and one cognitive technique to demonstrate and practise during the session.

When discussing acting in the opposite way to what the emotion is dictating, ask the participants to refer back to the chart created earlier and to note the behaviours typical of depression. Explain that when depressed, people typically want to withdraw and reduce their activity level and output. It is important to fight this impulse because when we act as this emotion is prompting us to do (e.g., withdrawing, going to bed, reducing responsibilities), we typically feel more depressed. When we act the opposite way to the emotion (e.g., interacting socially, getting things accomplished), we typically feel less depressed.

▶ **Distribute or turn to Handout 9-9: Practising Managing Sadness and Depression. Ask the participants to check off which approaches to managing their sadness they want to work on in the upcoming week, and to note how they will put each approach into practice.**

HOME PRACTICE

Ask the group members to complete Handout 9-9 by practising new methods of managing sadness and recording how it went. Ask that they read over Handout 9-2 and Handout 9-10 at home to remind them of effective methods of managing their sadness or depression.

FOR MORE INFORMATION

For more information on managing sadness and depression, see the following books:

Beck, A., Rush, J.A., Shaw, B.F., Emery, G. (1987). *Cognitive Therapy of Depression.* New York: Guilford Press.

Beck, J. (1995). *Cognitive Therapy: Basics and Beyond.* New York: Guilford Press.

Greenberger, D. & Padesky, C.A. (1995). *Mind Over Mood: Change How You Feel by Changing the Way You Think.* New York: Guilford Press.

Linehan, M. (1993). *Cognitive-Behavioural Therapy of Borderline Personality Disorder.* New York: Guilford Press.

Guilt and shame

UNDERSTANDING GUILT AND SHAME

▶ **Make three columns on a blackboard, whiteboard or flipchart. In the first column write the heading "Situations," in the second column write "Thoughts" and in the third column write "Responses."**

Ask the group members to identify when they feel guilty or ashamed in relation to their relative's problematic substance use, and what it is that causes them to have these feelings. Write their responses in the first column. Ask them then to identify what they think about in relation to the substance use when they are feeling guilty or ashamed, and write the responses in the second column. Finally, ask them to report what they experience physiologically and what they do behaviourally when they feel guilty or ashamed, and fill in the third column.

Ask the group members to define guilt and shame. (*Guilt* is a feeling of responsibility, remorse and/or self-reproach for having done something wrong. *Shame* is a strong sense of being unworthy, a disgrace, a disappointment and/or an embarrassment.)

Comment on the different components of guilt and shame and how they relate to each other: the environment, thoughts, physiology and behaviour. Distinguish between the thoughts associated with guilt and those associated with shame: guilt thoughts tend to involve "should have" statements, while shame thoughts tend to involve negative beliefs about oneself and the need to keep secret what the person finds shameful.

Like all emotions, guilt and shame are not "bad emotions." Discuss what purpose guilt and shame play in our lives. Point out that guilt and shame help us to determine when we have wronged others and need to make amends.

While guilt and shame are natural and sometimes helpful responses to situations (including how we have behaved), we may sometimes experience them unnecessarily or more strongly than the situation warrants. To determine the appropriateness of our reaction, we should assess the seriousness of the event or situation (including the harm done), and try to determine the degree to which we are responsible for it.

Tell the group members that to assess the seriousness of the event or situation, they can can ask themselves questions such as the following:
· Do other people consider this experience to be as serious as I do?
· Do some people consider it less serious? Why?
· How serious would I consider the experience if my best friend were responsible instead of me?
· How serious would I consider the experience if someone did it to me?

· Did I know ahead of time the meaning or consequences of my actions (or thoughts)? Based on what I knew at the time, do my current judgments still apply?

· Can any damage that occurred be corrected? How long will this take?

(Greenberger & Padesky, 1995, p. 201)

Second, to determine the degree of responsibility, encourage the participants to make use of the exercise in Handout 9-12: Determining Responsibility. Explain that many family members of people with substance use problems feel responsible for more than their share of problems.

MANAGING GUILT AND SHAME

▶ **Distribute or turn to Handout 9-11: Managing Guilt and Shame. Ask the group members to complete the question at the top of the handout.**

Now turn to Handout 9-2: Managing Emotions.

Discuss how these strategies, introduced in the previous session, would be relevant to managing guilt and shame.

▶ **When discussing how to manage guilt and shame specifically, turn again to Handout 9-11.**

Read through the strategies for dealing with guilt and shame.

▶ **Distribute or turn to Handout 9-12: Determining Responsibility.**

Go over the handout together. Ask one or more group members to identify something they feel guilty or ashamed of. As a group, help the person to determine the seriousness of the event or situation, and the degree to which he or she is responsible, using Handout 9-12 as a guide.

When discussing acting the opposite way to the emotion, explain that when people feel ashamed or guilty, they tend to be secretive, to treat themselves poorly, to talk negatively or abusively about themselves and/or to withdraw from others. To reduce feelings of guilt or shame, it is important to act opposite to this tendency (e.g., disclose the shameful secret, treat yourself well, challenge negative self-talk, interact socially).

▶ **Distribute or turn to Handout 9-13: Practising Managing Guilt and Shame. Ask the participants to check off which approaches to managing their guilt or shame they want to work on in the upcoming week, and to note how they will put each approach into practice.**

HOME PRACTICE

Ask the group members to complete Handout 9-13 by practising new methods of managing guilt and shame and recording how it went. Ask that they read over Handout 9-2 at home to remind them of effective methods of managing emotions.

FOR MORE INFORMATION

For more information on managing guilt and shame, see the following books:

Greenberger, D. & Padesky, C.A. (1995). *Mind Over Mood: Change How You Feel by Changing the Way You Think.* New York: Guilford Press.

Linehan, M. (1993). *Cognitive-Behavioural Therapy of Borderline Personality Disorder.* New York: Guilford Press.

Anger

UNDERSTANDING ANGER

Ask the group members to suggest words associated with anger (e.g., frustration, irritation, annoyance, rage), and note that in this session we are talking about any of these degrees of anger.

▶ **Make three columns on a blackboard, whiteboard or flipchart. In the first column write the heading "Situations," in the second column write "Thoughts" and in the third column write "Responses."**

Ask the group members to share when they feel angry in relation to their relative's problematic substance use, and what it is that causes them to feel angry. Write their responses in the first column. Ask them then to identify what they think about in relation to the substance use when they are feeling angry, and write the responses in the second column. Finally, ask them to report what they experience physiologically and what they do behaviourally when they feel angry, and fill in the third column.

Comment on the different components of anger and how they relate to each other: the environment, thoughts, physiology and behaviour. Emphasize the role of thoughts in anger. Suggest that the group members look for patterns in the second column of the chart in thinking associated with anger. Explain that when people feel angry, they tend to think that:

· others are being threatening or mean
· others are violating rules
· others are treating them (or someone else) unfairly.

Emphasize the physiology of anger. Ask the group members to describe how they feel when they experience mild, moderate and severe forms of anger. Encourage them to be mindful of becoming angry, so that they can intervene before reaching a high level of anger.

Anger often appears as a secondary emotion to the primary emotions of hurt and sadness. This makes the hurt difficult to deal with, because it is masked by the anger. The situation is made more complex by the fact that people often feel guilty about being angry; thus it is difficult for a person in this situation to deal with the anger. Both of these scenarios are common in families where someone has a substance use problem. Ask the group members for examples from their experience.

Emphasize that anger is often a healthy, normal reaction to situations and events, and that it can be a helpful emotion. Explain that the emotion itself is not "bad," and that it serves a purpose in communicating that something is wrong and needs to be fixed. Ask the group members for examples of when they have felt anger and what the anger has communicated to them.

MANAGING ANGER

▶ **Distribute or turn to Handout 9-14: Managing Anger. Ask the group members to complete the question at the top of the handout.**

Now turn to Handout 9-2: Managing Emotions.

Discuss how these strategies, introduced in the previous session, would be relevant to managing anger. When discussing how to reduce emotions, be sure not to invalidate group members' experiences of anger. Emphasize that even if anger is justified, we may still try to reduce it or channel it, so that we do not become overwhelmed by the anger and unable to respond constructively to the situation. Discuss what can happen when anger is not managed in a healthy or constructive way. For example, it can lead to:
· medical problems, such as hypertension, ulcers or headaches
· mental health problems, such as feelings of despair, helplessness or depression
· verbal or physical abuse of others
· resentment
· displacement (i.e., hurting someone else because you are not able to deal directly with the person with whom you are angry).

▶ **Distribute or turn to Handout 9-15: Cognitive-Behavioural Techniques for Managing Anger.**

Instruct group members on some of these strategies. Select one behavioural technique and one cognitive technique to demonstrate and practise during the session.

When discussing acting in the opposite way to what the emotion is dictating, ask the participants to refer back to the chart created earlier and to note the behaviours typical of anger. Explain that when angry, people typically want to lash out and hurt someone. It is important to fight this impulse because when we act as this emotion is prompting us to do (e.g., attacking, throwing objects), we typically feel more angry and do things that we later regret. When we act the opposite way to the emotion (e.g., withdrawing, taking time apart, breathing slowly), we typically feel less angry and can think through our options and respond more effectively.

▶ **Distribute or turn to Handout 9-16: Practising Managing Anger. Ask the participants to check off which approaches to managing their anger they want to work on in the upcoming week, and to note how they will put each approach into practice.**

HOME PRACTICE

Ask the group members to complete Handout 9-16 by practising new methods of managing their anger and recording how it went. Ask that they read over Handout 9-2 and Handout 9-15 at home to remind them of effective methods of managing anger.

FOR MORE INFORMATION

For more information on managing anger, see the following books:

McKay, M. & Rogers, P. (2000). *The Anger Control Workbook.* Oakland, CA: New Harbinger Publications.

References

American Psychiatric Association. (1994). *Diagnostic and Statistical Manual of Mental Disorders* (4th ed.). Washington, DC: Author.

Greenberger, D. & Padesky, C.A. (1995). *Mind Over Mood: Change How You Feel by Changing the Way You Think.* New York: Guilford Press.

Understanding our emotions

EMOTIONS SHOULD BE ACCEPTED
Emotions are a natural human phenomenon. We are more able to manage our emotions when we validate and accept them, rather than fighting, denying or continually suppressing them.

EMOTIONS MAY BE HIDDEN
Emotions may be hidden and yet may still affect our behaviour. We are able to manage our emotions better when we recognize them. We can often identify what we are feeling by pausing and paying attention to (being mindful of) our bodies, emotions and thoughts.

EMOTIONS VARY IN INTENSITY
Emotions often increase in intensity gradually. We are more able to deal with emotions at low intensities, so it is helpful to pay continual attention to (be mindful of) our bodies, emotions and thoughts, and to deal with emotions as soon as we become aware of them.

EMOTIONS SERVE A PURPOSE
One purpose of emotions is to convey to ourselves and others how we are doing and what might need to be changed in a certain situation.

EMOTIONS MAY NOT OCCUR ALONE
We may feel multiple emotions when dealing with complex situations.

EMOTIONS MAY BE PRIMARY OR SECONDARY
Secondary emotions often mask underlying primary emotions and complicate how we understand and manage our feelings. For example:
· anger can mask feeling hurt or disappointed
· anxiety can mask feeling sad or depressed
· shame can mask feeling anxious or worried
· anger at ourselves can mask feeling angry at someone else.

    We need to determine what is our primary emotion.

EMOTIONS MAY BE MORE INTENSE WHEN WE ARE PHYSICALLY VULNERABLE

Emotions may be more difficult to deal with and seem more intense when we are physically vulnerable. We need to take care of ourselves by getting proper health care, sleep, food and exercise. We also need to manage or reduce our own substance use, because substances usually increase our vulnerability to emotions and prevent us from dealing with emotions effectively.

EMOTIONS MAY BE EXHAUSTING AND OVERWHELMING

We can take breaks from dealing with difficult emotions by temporarily distracting ourselves. For example, we can exercise, watch a movie, take a shower or read a book.

EMOTIONS CAN BE TOLERATED AND MANAGED

Emotions come and go and change their intensity over time. We can ride emotional experiences like a surfer rides waves. We can remind ourselves while experiencing emotions that the emotion will pass. We might be able to help ourselves tolerate difficult emotions by engaging in soothing activities (e.g., taking a bath, going for a walk, sipping herbal tea, listening to music).

EMOTIONS ARE MORE EASILY ADDRESSED WITH THE SUPPORT OF TRUSTED OTHERS

We can better deal with our emotions when we experience the validation and comfort of friends, family members, professionals or other group members. We do not have to manage alone.

EMOTIONS ARE INTERCONNECTED WITH OUR THOUGHTS AND BEHAVIOURS

How we feel, think and behave relate to and influence one another. Emotions are influenced by our thoughts, so we can change our emotions by changing our thoughts. Likewise, emotions are influenced by our behaviour, so we can change our emotions by changing our behaviour. We can often succeed at changing our emotion if we act the opposite way to how we feel.

EMOTIONS CAN BE REDUCED OR CHANGED

Emotions are valid, yet we may want to reduce the intensity or change them because:

· they may interfere with our health (e.g., we feel so anxious that we are chronically experiencing physiological symptoms)

· they may keep us from taking appropriate action (e.g., we feel so much rage that we are not able to think clearly enough to devise a plan to improve the situation)
· they may be too intense and overwhelming (e.g., we feel so sad that we feel helpless and hopeless about our situation)
· they may not be warranted by a situation (e.g., we might feel ashamed of our family member's substance use).

EMOTIONS CAN SIGNAL THAT WE NEED PROFESSIONAL HELP

We may need to seek mental health treatment for problems with anxiety, depression, shame or anger.

Managing emotions

BE MINDFUL OF YOUR EMOTIONS

ACKNOWLEDGE YOUR EMOTION
Pay attention to what you are feeling and when you are feeling that way.

ACCEPT THE FACT THAT YOU ARE EXPERIENCING A PARTICULAR EMOTION
Do not tell yourself that you should not be feeling that way. Do not fight or try to suppress the emotion.

PAY ATTENTION TO YOUR EMOTION
Notice how you are feeling, thinking and behaving.

CONSIDER WHAT THE EMOTION IS COMMUNICATING TO YOU
Determine if there is some action that you need to take. For example:
· What is my anger telling me about the situation? (E.g., does it indicate that I am tolerating too much from my partner?)
· What is my sadness telling me about myself? (E.g., does it indicate that I am neglecting myself?)
· What is my anxiety telling me about my life? (E.g., does it indicate that I am taking on too much responsibility?)

After becoming mindful of your emotions, you may choose to experience them or to reduce their intensity (see below).

EXPERIENCE YOUR EMOTIONS

EXPRESS YOUR EMOTIONS
Express your feelings by emoting (e.g., crying, laughing), talking about the feeling (e.g., sharing it with a friend), writing about it (e.g., in a journal) or artistically conveying the feeling (e.g., playing music, making art).

SURF YOUR EMOTIONS
Remind yourself that the intensity of your emotion will shift over time and that you will soon feel better.

NURTURE YOURSELF THROUGH YOUR EMOTIONS

Be kind and caring to yourself. For example, have a bath, get a massage, eat a favourite dessert, snuggle up with a good book, pray, accept the loving kindness of a friend.

NOTE: When allowing yourself to experience your feelings, do so cautiously and in a controlled manner. If your emotion seems too overwhelming, harmful or gets in the way of what you want to do, use the techniques discussed below to reduce the intensity of the emotion.

REDUCE THE INTENSITY OF YOUR EMOTIONS

DISTRACT YOURSELF FROM THE EMOTION

For example, watch a movie, go out with friends, wash dishes, play sports, play chess, meditate.

EXAMINE AND CHANGE YOUR THOUGHTS ASSOCIATED WITH THE EMOTION

For example:
· Fear: If you are assuming the worst-case scenario, try to determine realistically if that will occur, and then consider a more likely future scenario.
· Depression: If you are focusing on negative things in your life, try to be more balanced in your thinking and also notice what is going well.
· Anxiety or depression: If you believe that you will fail, try to remember times when you have succeeded, and use these memories to encourage yourself.
· Anger: If you are dwelling on all the negative characteristics of a person and all the ways he or she has wronged you, try to be more balanced in your thinking and also acknowledge what you like about the person and what that person has done well.

ACT OPPOSITE TO WHAT YOUR EMOTION IS TELLING YOU TO DO

If an emotion makes you to want to act in a particular way, resist it and act opposite to it. You will not only be acting differently, you will also begin to feel different.

For example:
· If you feel depressed and want to stay in bed all day, get out of bed, have a shower, get dressed, eat and go out.

- If you feel guilty and ashamed and want to hide away and be secretive, visit friends and tell them what is going on. Expose the shameful secret (perhaps about your relative's substance use).
- If you feel anxious about communicating your conflict with a relative and instead want to sweep it under the rug, push yourself to have this conversation.
- If you feel angry and want to yell or throw things at your relative, remove yourself from the situation and take time to calm down before addressing the matter.

LET GO OF THE EMOTION OR THOUGHTS

For example:
- Write down your emotions or thoughts and file them away.
- Mentally observe yourself letting go of the emotion or thoughts.
- Do something relaxing to let go of physical and emotional tension.
- Pray and give your emotions or thoughts to God (or a higher power).

FOR MORE INFORMATION

For more information on these techniques for dealing with emotions, which are based on cognitive-behavioural therapy, dialectical behaviour therapy and mindfulness, please refer to Handout 9-17: Books for Managing Emotions.

Managing difficult emotions

What have you felt this week in relation to your relative's substance use?

_____

_____

_____

Which of these emotions have you had difficulty managing?

_____

_____

_____

How have you been managing these emotions?

_____

_____

STRATEGIES FOR DEALING WITH EMOTIONS

Indicate which of the following strategies you have been using successfully in managing your emotions.

BEING MINDFUL OF YOUR EMOTIONS

· Acknowledge your emotion
· Accept your emotion
· Pay attention to your emotion
· Consider what your emotion is communicating to you

EXPERIENCING YOUR EMOTIONS

· Express your emotion
· Surf the emotion—remind yourself that the emotion's intensity will increase and decrease like a wave
· Nurture yourself as you experience the emotion

REDUCING THE INTENSITY OF YOUR EMOTIONS

· Distract yourself from your emotion
· Examine and change your thoughts
· Act opposite to your emotion
· Let go of your emotion

Practising managing emotions

The emotion I would like to practise managing this week:

_____

The strategies I will use to manage the emotion this week:

_____

_____

_____

In the table below, record your experience this week of using these strategies in at least one situation.

	FIRST SITUATION	SECOND SITUATION
What happened?		
How did you feel?		
How did you manage the feeling?		
How did you feel afterward?		

Managing anxiety

What worries, anxieties or fears do you have that are related to your relative's substance use?

_____

_____

_____

_____

STRATEGIES FOR DEALING WITH ANXIETY

Check off the strategies that you use successfully to manage your anxiety:

- ☐ Acknowledge and accept your anxiety
- ☐ Determine if you can make any changes to reduce what it is you fear (if so, set goals and take steps to do so)
- ☐ Distract yourself from your anxiety
- ☐ Help your body and mind to relax (e.g., listen to music, focus on your breathing, relax your muscles, exercise)
- ☐ Expose yourself to the fear (e.g., feel the fear and do what you dread anyway)
- ☐ Examine and change your thoughts (e.g., weigh the evidence, engage in positive self-talk)
- ☐ Contain your worrying (e.g., practise thought stopping, set aside worrying time, write down worries)
- ☐ Let go of your worries (e.g., pray, meditate, accept uncertainty)

Practising managing anxiety

Check off the approaches you would like to use to deal with your anxiety and, for each approach, note how you will do so.

☐ Acknowledge and accept your anxiety

_____

_____

☐ Determine what you can change

_____

_____

☐ Distract yourself from your anxiety

_____

_____

☐ Help your body and mind to relax

_____

_____

☐ Expose yourself to your fear

_____

_____

☐ Examine and change your thoughts

_____

_____

☐ Contain your worrying

_____

_____

☐ Practise letting go of the anxiety and worries

_____

In the table below, record your experience this week using these strategies in at least one situation.

	FIRST SITUATION	SECOND SITUATION
What happened?		
How did you feel?		
How did you manage the feeling?		
How did you feel afterward?		

Cognitive-behavioural techniques for managing anxiety

BEHAVIOURAL TECHNIQUES

Breathing training

Regularly practise the following breathing exercises at times when you do not feel particularly anxious. Continue this practice until you are able to use these strategies when you feel more anxious.

MINDFUL BREATHING

Pay attention to your breathing. Concentrate on the breath going in and out. When you become distracted (particularly by worrisome thoughts), return your attention to your breathing.

ABDOMINAL BREATHING

Put your hand on your abdomen. Feel your abdomen (not your chest or shoulders) expanding and contracting. Abdominal breathing is more relaxing than chest breathing. If you notice that your abdomen is not moving, try lying down and breathing; then, when you have mastered this, practise breathing in the same way when standing.

SLOW BREATHING

Pay attention to the speed at which you are breathing. If it is fast, try to slow down your breathing, particularly when exhaling. Try to make your breathing as calm and natural as possible. You might want to internally recite the word *calm* as you exhale.

Relaxation training

Regularly practise the following physical relaxation exercises at times when you are not particularly anxious. Continue this practice until you are able to relax physically when you feel more anxious.

PROGRESSIVE MUSCLE RELAXATION

Sit or lie in a comfortable position. Start by tensing and then relaxing your toes or fingers. Notice the difference between how they feel when tense and how they feel when relaxed. Repeat this process, progressing through your whole body.

FOCUSED RELAXATION

Sit or lie in a comfortable position. Start by paying attention to your toes or fingers. Notice if they are tense. If they are, make them relax (it may help to imagine them becoming heavier). Apply this process to the rest of your body parts.

LISTENING TO MUSIC

Sit or lie in a comfortable position. Listen to a piece of music that you find relaxing. Use the music in combination with the method described under "Focused Relaxation." Alternatively, focus on the music and allow yourself to become absorbed in it. If you become distracted, return your focus to the music.

Exposing yourself to the fear

When you want to avoid doing something (e.g., imposing a limit on your family member, sharing your feelings, asking for help) or to avoid a situation (e.g., a neighbourhood event, a family dinner) because you feel anxious, force yourself to confront it. Assuming that you are safe, do the thing you fear. Assuming that you are safe, stay in the place where you are anxious. The more often you do the thing you fear or the longer you stay in an anxiety-provoking situation, the more likely it is that your anxiety will decrease. This reduction in anxiety will help you feel less anxious when facing similar tasks or situations in the future.

COGNITIVE TECHNIQUES

Decatastrophizing

Notice what negative predictions you are making about the future. For example:

· "If I tell my friends about my partner's substance use, they might think that I'm a bad person."
· "If I set limits on my son, he may become angry with me."
· "If I don't call my partner's boss and lie about why she is late for work, my partner may lose her job."

    Ask yourself the following questions:

· What if my fears actually come true?
· How could I cope with _____ if it were to occur?
· Would _____ really be as terrible as I think?

· Does this really matter in the big scheme of things?
· Will I care about this a month / a year from now?

Weighing the evidence

Notice what negative predictions you are making about the future. For example:

· "If I tell my son that he can't drink in the house, I'm afraid he will leave and never come back again."
· "If I tell my friends about my partner's substance use, they might stop visiting me."
· "If I stop giving my daughter money, I'm afraid she will start trading sex for money."

Examine what evidence you have that these predictions will come true or that they will not come true.

Using the first example:

· Provide evidence *for* this prediction:
  - My son does get very angry when I talk to him about his drinking, and on a few occasions he has stormed out and not returned until the next day.
· Provide evidence *against* this prediction:
  - I have had to set limits about other things with my son and, although he has become angry, he has continued to remain in our family and our home.
  - I have a friend who told her son that he could not use substances in the house or come home while high, and he did not leave his family.
  - I have suggested in the past that my son move out and he refuses to do so.
  - I believe that setting this limit with my son demonstrates that I love him, and I believe he will be more likely to stay if he feels that we care about him.
· Choose a more realistic way of thinking:
  - It is possible that my son will leave temporarily, but that might not be a bad thing and it seems highly likely that he will return. Setting this limit may even help me not become resentful and exhausted, which may protect our relationship in the long run. Imposing this limit may also set my son on a path to recovery, because he will have to work harder to use substances and will have to face the consequences of his substance use.

Positive self-talk

Give yourself words of encouragement and words that will build your confidence. For example:

· "I can do this. I am a competent, smart woman. I have thought through this situation and come up with a good solution. I can communicate my intentions to my partner. I know that I am doing the right thing. I am normal in how I am feeling and responding."

Reason with yourself. For example, tell yourself:

· "I can manage if he is angry with me."
· "It is OK if I am anxious and become flustered while confronting her."
· "Everyone does not have to like my plan."

Thought stopping

· Notice yourself thinking the unwanted anxious thought.
· Say to yourself "Stop!" or "Get out of here!" or "Leave!"
· Repeat this process as many times as necessary. Eventually you will convince yourself that you do not have to put up with such worrisome thoughts.

Mindful contained worrying

· Set aside a certain time of the day, a certain place and a certain amount of time for worrying.
· During this time, pay attention to your worries. You may even want to write them down. Examine whether you can do anything about your worries. If you can, make a plan to stop the worrisome event from occurring. If you cannot, practise letting go of it. You may wish to do this visually (e.g., imagine the worries floating down a river or falling through a sieve), physically (e.g., crossing off or ripping up the worries you have written down) or spiritually (e.g., giving your worries to God or a higher power).
· If you worry outside of your designated worry time, use thought stopping to stop yourself. Remind yourself that you will get plenty of time to worry later.

Accepting uncertainty

· Acknowledge that you do not know the future and can never know with certainty all the risks involved in an action and its possible outcomes.
· Tell yourself that you can tolerate uncertainty and risk.

FOR MORE INFORMATION

For more information on these techniques for dealing with anxiety, and other techniques based on cognitive-behavioural therapy, dialectical behaviour therapy and mindfulness, please refer to Handout 9-17: Books for Managing Emotions.

Managing sadness and depression

What have you felt sad or depressed about in relation to your relative's substance use?

_____

_____

_____

_____

STRATEGIES FOR DEALING WITH SADNESS AND DEPRESSION

Check off the strategies that you use successfully to manage your sadness or depression:

- ☐ Acknowledge and accept your sadness or depression
- ☐ Determine if there is anything you can do to change what it is that is making you sad (if so, set goals and take steps to do so)
- ☐ Distract yourself from the sadness or depression (e.g., watch a comedy, volunteer, read a book, go for a walk)
- ☐ Be active (e.g., get out of bed, engage in positive events or activities, go for a walk, play sports, exercise)
- ☐ Be social (e.g., phone friends, go out to dinner, visit family, attend a religious service)
- ☐ Be productive (e.g., volunteer, clean your house, go to work)
- ☐ Examine and change your thoughts (e.g., challenge hopeless and negative statements, engage in positive self-talk)
- ☐ Nurture yourself (e.g., take a bath, get a haircut, drink tea, listen to music, get a massage)

Practising managing sadness and depression

Check off the approaches you would like to use to deal with your sadness or depression and, for each approach, note how you will do so.

☐ Acknowledge and accept your sadness or depression

_____

_____

☐ Determine what you can change

_____

☐ Distract yourself from the sadness or depression

_____

_____

☐ Be active

_____

_____

☐ Be social

_____

_____

☐ Be productive

_____

_____

☐ Examine and change your thoughts

_____

_____

☐ Nurture yourself

_____

In the table below, record your experience this week using these strategies in at least one situation.

	FIRST SITUATION	SECOND SITUATION
What happened?		
How did you feel?		
How did you manage the feeling?		
How did you feel afterward?		

Cognitive-behavioural techniques for managing depression

BEHAVIOURAL TECHNIQUE: ACTIVITY SCHEDULING

Schedule your days and weeks so they are as close as possible to your behaviour and schedule when you are not depressed (unless you have been overscheduled and overworked). Activity scheduling is most important when you least feel like being active. You may feel like staying in bed, but if you do, you will probably only become more depressed. By engaging in nurturing, fun, physical, productive and social activities, you will feel less depressed. If you are currently doing very few activities, you may need to start with small additions to your schedule and work up to a more active schedule.

PRACTISE REGULAR SELF-CARE

Make a list of self-care activities that you have previously engaged in (e.g., showering, grooming, eating, stretching, receiving massages, getting needed medical, dental or mental health care, getting a haircut, having baths). Choose which of these you will continue or pursue. Schedule when to do each of these.

HAVE FUN

Make a list of activities that you have previously enjoyed (e.g., cooking, playing a sport, watching movies, playing cards, painting). Choose at least one activity you will continue or pursue (even if you are not currently interested in doing it). Plan to do one of these each day.

EXERCISE

Make a list of forms of physical activity that you have previously engaged in (e.g., walking, swimming, dancing, playing hockey, practising yoga). Choose at least one form of exercise you will continue or pursue. Schedule one of these each day.

BE PRODUCTIVE

Make a list of responsibilities that you have previously had (e.g., walking the dog, vacuuming, helping children with homework, going to work, writing letters, attending board meetings, volunteering). Choose which of these to continue or pursue, and plan a time when you will do it.

BE SOCIAL

Make a list of people whom you have previously interacted with and social engagements that you have previously enjoyed (e.g., going out for dinner; going to a church, synagogue or mosque; attending exercise classes; playing sports; attending parties; shopping; volunteering; talking on the phone). Choose which of these you would like to pursue and with whom. Schedule a time to do each of these.

COGNITIVE TECHNIQUE: CHALLENGING DISTORTED THINKING

Our thinking can affect how we feel. Sometimes our thinking causes us to be depressed. Use the following method to change your thinking so that you feel less depressed.

1. Identify when you are upset and what is upsetting you.

2. Notice how you are feeling.

3. Notice what you are thinking. Ask yourself what you are saying to yourself about the problem, about you, about others and about the future.

4. Notice if your thoughts are unbalanced, unrealistic, unfounded or excessively negative.

5. Consider what evidence exists to support and to counter this way of thinking.

6. Create and substitute a more rational way of thinking about the situation.

FOR MORE INFORMATION

For more information on these techniques for dealing with depression, and other techniques based on cognitive-behavioural therapy, dialectical behaviour therapy and mindfulness, please refer to Handout 9-17: Books for Managing Emotions.

Managing guilt and shame

What have you felt guilty or ashamed about in relation to your relative's substance use?

_____

_____

_____

_____

STRATEGIES FOR DEALING WITH GUILT AND SHAME

· Acknowledge and accept your feelings of guilt or shame.
· Determine if your feelings of guilt or shame are warranted by the situation.
· Determine the seriousness of the situation or problem.
· Determine your responsibility for the situation or problem.

If it is *appropriate* that you should feel guilty or ashamed, and to the degree that you do:
· make amends to the person you have wronged
· forgive yourself.

If it is *inappropriate* that you should feel guilty or ashamed, or if your guilt or shame is out of proportion to the situation, or if your guilt or shame persists despite your making amends:
· let go of your guilt or shame, and of what you are not responsible for
· challenge any blaming or abusive thinking about yourself
· distract yourself from the guilt or shame (e.g., go swimming, watch a movie, bake, visit with a friend)
· act the opposite way to the emotion (e.g., nurture yourself, hold your head up, visit people, share your guilty or shameful secret).

Determining responsibility

1. Identify a negative event or situation about which you feel guilty or ashamed.

_____

_____

_____

2. List the people and circumstances that have contributed to the situation.

_____

_____

_____

3. Divide the pie below into slices, and label the slices with the names of the people or circumstances on your list. Assign bigger portions to people or circumstances that you think have greater responsibility for the event or situation.

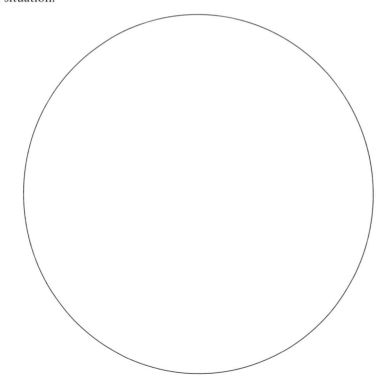

4. When you have finished, notice how much responsibility is yours alone and how much you share with others.

5. How does this responsibility pie affect your feelings of guilt or shame about this event or situation?

_____

_____

_____

Adapted from Greenberger, D. & Padesky, C.A. (1995). *Mind Over Mood: Change How You Feel by Changing the Way You Think.* New York: Guilford Press.

Practising managing guilt and shame

Check off the approaches you would like to use to deal with your guilt or shame and, for each approach, note how you will do so.

☐ Acknowledge and accept your guilt or shame

_____

_____

☐ Determine if the guilt or shame is warranted by the situation

_____

_____

☐ Make amends to the person you have wronged

_____

_____

☐ Forgive yourself

_____

_____

☐ Let go of guilt, shame or responsibility

_____

_____

☐ Distract yourself from the guilt or shame

_____

_____

☐ Challenge negative thinking about yourself

_____

_____

☐ Nurture yourself

_____

_____

☐ Act the opposite way to what the guilt and shame are telling you to do

_____

_____

☐ Expose the guilty or shameful secret

_____

_____

In the table below, record your experience this week of using these strategies in at least one situation.

	FIRST SITUATION	SECOND SITUATION
What happened?		
How did you feel?		
How did you manage the feeling?		
How did you feel afterward?		

Managing anger

What have you felt angry about in relation to your relative's substance use?

_____

_____

_____

_____

STRATEGIES FOR DEALING WITH ANGER

Check off the strategies that you use successfully to manage your anger:

- ☐ Acknowledge and accept your anger
- ☐ Determine what the anger is telling you and consider what you can change to reduce this source of your anger
- ☐ Distract yourself from your anger
- ☐ Act the opposite way to what the anger is telling you to do (e.g., the impulse to attack)
- ☐ Take time out until you have calmed down (e.g., take a walk, count, focus on breathing)
- ☐ Calm your body and mind (e.g., relax your muscles, exercise or focus on your breathing)
- ☐ Examine and change your thoughts:
  - ☐ reduce judgment
  - ☐ increase empathy
  - ☐ check assumptions and attributions
  - ☐ forgive

Cognitive-behavioural techniques for managing anger

BEHAVIOURAL TECHNIQUES

Taking time out

Remove yourself physically from the situation (e.g., leave the room, car, house, restaurant, conversation) to calm down. Do not return to the situation until you feel calmer.

Remove yourself psychologically from the situation. You may wish to do one of the breathing or relaxation exercises below, or you may distract yourself by counting, performing calculations, internally reciting something or engaging in a physical activity. Do not return to the situation until you feel calmer.

Breathing training

Regularly practise the following breathing exercises at times when you are not particularly angry. Continue practising until you are able to use these strategies when you feel more angry.

MINDFUL BREATHING

Pay attention to your breathing. Concentrate on the breath going in and out. When you become distracted (particularly by angry thoughts), return your attention to your breathing.

ABDOMINAL BREATHING

Put your hand on your abdomen. Feel your abdomen (not your chest or shoulders) expanding and contracting. Abdominal breathing is more relaxing than chest breathing. If you notice that your abdomen is not moving, try lying down and breathing; then, when you have mastered this, practise breathing in the same way when standing.

SLOW BREATHING

Pay attention to the speed at which you are breathing. If it is fast, try to slow down your breathing, particularly when exhaling. Try to make your breathing as calm and natural as possible. You might want to internally recite the word *calm* as you exhale.

Relaxation training

Regularly practise the following physical relaxation exercises at times when you are not particularly angry. Continue practising them until you are able to relax physically when you feel more angry.

PROGRESSIVE MUSCLE RELAXATION

Sit or lie in a comfortable position. Start by tensing and then relaxing your toes or fingers. Notice the difference between how they feel when tense and how they feel when relaxed. Repeat this process, progressing through your whole body.

FOCUSED RELAXATION

Sit or lie in a comfortable position. Start by paying attention to your toes or fingers. Notice if they feel tense. If they do, try to make them relax. (It may help to imagine them becoming heavier.) Apply this process to all your body parts.

COGNITIVE TECHNIQUES

Reducing judgment

Notice the judging thoughts that you are having about your relative. Judgments often come in the form of name-calling. For example:
· "He's such a lazy slob."
· "She thinks only of herself. She's so selfish."

Try to identify the behaviour that you dislike, without judging your relative. Try to let the judgments go. For example:
· "I don't like it when he leaves his dishes and clothes lying around."
· "I don't like it when she doesn't ask me if I have already made plans."

Try not to dwell on about everything that you dislike about the person, or every way in which he or she has wronged you in the past.

Increasing empathy

Try to understand what your relative is feeling or thinking, and what he or she may be struggling with. For example:
· "I know he's under a lot of stress right now because of his exams."
· "I can understand that she was very disappointed and angry because of my decision."

Note that empathy can help you to understand, but should not be used to excuse your relative's behaviour.

Checking assumptions and attributions

Notice what assumptions and attributions (the reasons you believe something happened) you are making about your relative. For example:

· "He's so inconsiderate. He knew that I was having a bad day, but he chose to go out drinking anyway just to punish me."

· "She got drunk just to get back at me and embarrass me in front of my friends."

Do not assume that your assumptions and attributions are fact. Think of alternative explanations for your relative's behaviour. Try not to personalize his or her behaviour or assume deliberate, malicious intent. If necessary, check out your assumptions with the person.

Forgiving

When it seems reasonable and possible, try to forgive your relative for past wrongdoings. Forgiveness can allow you to let go of unpleasant resentments and to deal with one behaviour at a time. Remember that forgiveness does not excuse or erase past harms, nor does it remove the consequences of harm. You can acknowledge that what was done was wrong, hurtful or damaging, and yet forgive the person who was responsible. There will be situations in which you may forgive easily, but at other times you will need time to heal before you can forgive.

FOR MORE INFORMATION

For more information on these and other anger-management techniques based on cognitive-behavioural therapy, dialectical behaviour therapy and mindfulness, please refer to Handout 9-17: Books for Managing Emotions.

Practising managing anger

Check off the approaches you would like to use to deal with your anger and, for each approach, note how you will do so.

☐ Acknowledge and accept your anger

_____

_____

☐ Determine what you can change

_____

_____

☐ Distract yourself from your anger

_____

_____

☐ Take time out

_____

_____

☐ Calm your body and mind

_____

_____

☐ Examine and change your thoughts:
  ☐ reduce judgment
  ☐ increase empathy
  ☐ check assumptions and attributions
  ☐ forgive

_____

_____

_____

In the table below, record your experience this week of using these strategies in at least one situation.

	FIRST SITUATION	SECOND SITUATION
What happened?		
How did you feel?		
How did you manage the feeling?		
How did you feel afterward?		

Books for managing emotions

Addis, M. & Martell, C. (2004). *Overcoming Depression One Step at a Time: The New Behavioral Activation Approach to Getting Your Life Back.* Oakland, CA: New Harbinger Publications.

Antony, M. & Swinson, R. (2000). *The Shyness and Social Anxiety Workbook.* Oakland, CA: New Harbinger Publications.

Burns, D. (1991). *The Feeling Good Handbook.* New York: Penguin.

Copeland, M.E. (2002). *The Depression Workbook: A Guide for Living with Depression and Manic Depression* (2nd ed.). Oakland, CA: New Harbinger Publications.

Davis, M., Robbins-Eshelman, E. & Davis, M. (1995). *The Relaxation and Stress Reduction Workbook.* Oakland, CA: New Harbinger Publications.

Greenberger, D. & Padesky, C. (1995). *Mind Over Mood: Change How You Feel by Changing the Way You Think.* New York: Guilford Press.

Hallowell, E. (1998). *Worry: Hope and Help for a Common Condition.* New York: Ballantine Books.

Marra, T. (2004). *Depressed and Anxious: The Dialectical Behavior Therapy Workbook for Overcoming Depression and Anxiety.* Oakland, CA: New Harbinger Publications.

McKay, M. & Rogers, P. (2000). *The Anger Control Workbook.* Oakland, CA: New Harbinger Publications.

Zinn, J.K. (2001). *Full Catastrophe Living: How to Cope with Stress, Pain and Illness Using Mindfulness Meditation.* New York: Random House.

Communicating effectively with a person who has a substance use problem

OBJECTIVES

· to emphasize the importance of effective communication
· to help group members become aware of barriers to good communication
· to teach group members effective listening and speaking skills
· to encourage group members to practise more effective listening and speaking skills in the session and at home

HANDOUTS

10-1: Barriers to Effective Communication
10-2: Tips for Communicating with People Who Have a Substance Use Problem
10-3: Practising Communication
10-4: Examples of Active Listening
10-5: Practising More Active Listening
10-6: Effective Speaking
10-7: Examples of Effective Speaking
10-8: Practising More Effective Speaking

· Opening and announcements (approx. 5 min.)
· Check-in and review of last week's home practice (approx. 30 min.)
· Teaching and discussion (approx. 60 min.)
· Assigning of next week's home practice (approx. 5 min.)
· Closing (approx. 5 min.)

NOTE: This module is divided into two parts, each of which should be presented in a separate session. If you only have time to offer one of these sessions, we advise that you offer Part 1.

Part 1

TEACHING AND DISCUSSION

Benefits of effective communication

Ask the group members about the benefits of working on improving communication, which include:

· a greater likelihood of being heard
· a greater likelihood of getting what you want
· a greater likelihood of hearing and understanding the person with a substance use problem.
· a greater ability to express feelings, needs and desires
· a greater sense of integrity (as a result of not resorting to unhealthy communication)
· a greater ability to set limits
· a greater ability to be supportive and helpful
· less likelihood of ineffective fighting or nagging
· less hostility in the relationship
· less stress.

Explain to group members that improving communication skills is likely to increase their effectiveness in getting what they want and enhance their relationship. Nevertheless, caution them that this positive outcome is not guaranteed. Emphasize that they may not get the response that they want even if they communicate effectively, however, they will feel better about themselves. For example, most people do not feel good yelling at or nagging a family member.

Barriers to effective communication

Ask the group members to talk about what often happens when they try to communicate with the person in their family who has a substance use problem. What prevents them from communicating effectively?

▶ **Write the responses on a blackboard, whiteboard or flipchart.**

Then distribute or turn to Handout 10-1: Barriers to Effective Communication.

Briefly discuss the barriers listed on the handout—those pertaining to the person with a substance use problem and those pertaining to the other family members. Highlight the barriers not already mentioned by the group. Solicit examples from the group members.

Effective communication skills

Ask the group members to discuss how they have learned to communicate with the person who has a substance use problem.

▶ **Distribute or turn to Handout 10-2: Tips for Communicating with People Who Have a Substance Use Problem, and briefly discuss each tip.**

Ask the group members to indicate which of these approaches they use successfully, and which ones they need to work on. Tell them to place a check mark beside those they do well and to circle those that they need to improve.

▶ **Distribute or turn to Handout 10-3: Practising Communication. Direct the group members to complete the first four questions during the session.**

HOME PRACTICE

Ask the participants to try this intended communication at home this week and to record how it went.

Part 2

TEACHING AND DISCUSSION

Active listening

▶ **Distribute or turn to Handout 10-4: Examples of Active Listening.**

Talk about the elements of active listening and why we use them:
- Listen attentively—to demonstrate listening and interest; to encourage the speaker to continue.
- Clarify—not to assume the meaning behind words, but to understand accurately what someone else has said; to demonstrate attentiveness and care about what has been said.
- Paraphrase—to demonstrate attentiveness and care about what has been said; to communicate what you heard so that if you misunderstood, you can be corrected.
- Validate—to demonstrate understanding; to demonstrate that what the other person has said, done or experienced makes sense to you; to reduce defensiveness; to reduce emotional intensity.

Read the examples on the handout and do one or more role plays, either as a group or in pairs. We suggest that a facilitator demonstrate the exercise before asking for volunteers.

The most difficult element of active listening is to provide validating responses, particularly with people who have a substance use problem. Therefore we suggest that in addition to partner role plays, you have someone play the role of a person who has substance use problems, and the group as a whole suggest validating responses.

▶ **Distribute or turn to Handout 10-5: Practising More Active Listening. Ask each group member to complete the first part of the handout and to tell the group which skill he or she has chosen to work on.**

Effective speaking

▶ **Distribute or turn to Handout 10-6: Effective Speaking.**

Briefly discuss the DESC framework, presented in the handout. Emphasize the purpose of this framework: that it helps speakers avoid criticism and contempt, and increases the likelihood of the listener hearing what is being said and not becoming defensive. Ask for volunteers to read the examples on the handout.

Ask the group members to come up with examples of their own and to read them to the group.

▶ **Distribute or turn to Handout 10-7: Examples of Effective Speaking, and encourage the group members to read it at home.**

Then distribute or turn to Handout 10-8: Practising More Effective Speaking, and ask the group members to spend about five minutes completing the first part.

Ask the participants to share their plan with the group.

HOME PRACTICE

Ask the group members to work on a listening skill once during the week with their relative who has a substance use problem. Also ask them to try speaking to their relative using the DESC framework once during the week.

FOR MORE INFORMATION

For more information on the DESC framework, please refer to the following book:

Bower, S. & Bower, A. (2004). *Asserting Yourself: A Practical Guide for Positive Change.* Cambridge, MA: Da Capo Press.

Barriers to effective communication

How people with substance use problems contribute to communication difficulties:

· **substance use:** being preoccupied, absent, confused, agitated, inattentive or emotionally vulnerable due to substance use, the urge to get hold of substances, or withdrawal from substances

· **recovery:** being preoccupied and exhausted by recovery, and having difficulty coping (particularly with emotions) because of not using substances

· **denial:** not being ready to deal with substance use problems; reacting to challenges or suggestions by being defensive and asking to be left alone

· **shame:** being aware of the problem, but feeling shame and thus fearing communication about the substance use

· **emotional vulnerability:** being hungry, tired, physically unwell, mentally unwell or stressed

· **need for skills improvement:** more teaching and practice in how to listen, validate, express emotions, state requests and say no.

How family members contribute to communication problems:

· **minimization:** not wanting to acknowledge the extent or severity of the problem, perhaps because of fear, shame or stigma

· **walking on eggshells:** fearing that what you say might result in an intense emotional reaction, abuse, risky behaviour, and/or the person using substances or relapsing

· **resignation and hopelessness:** previous unsuccessful experiences in communicating with the person

· **belief in mind-reading:** believing that the person with a substance use problem should already know how you are thinking and feeling, and how you would like him or her to behave

· **emotional vulnerability:** being hungry, tired, physically unwell, mentally unwell or stressed

· **need for skills improvement:** more teaching and practice in how to listen, validate, express emotions, state requests and say no.

Tips for communicating with people who have a substance use problem

CHOOSE AN APPROPRIATE TIME
Choose a time:
· when the person is not using substances
· when you and the other person are both calm and not emotionally vulnerable
· when neither of you is in a hurry.

CHOOSE A NEUTRAL PLACE
Choose a place:
· that is not associated with using substances or with fights
· where you will be safe.

LISTEN AND VALIDATE
· Listen attentively to the other person.
· Do not interrupt.
· Do not judge.
· Paraphrase what you have heard and seek clarification when necessary.
· Verbalize the feelings, thoughts and actions of the other person that make sense to you.
· Communicate understanding of the other person's perspective.

TAKE RESPONSIBILITY
· Use "I" statements when talking about your feelings and needs.
· Acknowledge your part in the problem.
· Offer to contribute to solving the problem and to compromise when possible.

BE SPECIFIC
· Avoid sweeping negative statements about the person who has a substance use problem.
· Avoid general statements such as "you never" or "you always."
· State how you would like the person to behave.

BE POSITIVE AND CALM
· Word your requests in a positive way.
· Speak in a calm tone of voice.
· Avoid critical, sarcastic, demeaning or blaming remarks.

· Suggest what you would like the person to do, rather than what you do *not* want the person do.

BE FIRM

· Be a "broken record" if necessary.
· Stay focused on your goal (do not let emotions or arguments derail you).

Practising communication

Indicate which of the following tips you would like to practise:
- ☐ choosing an appropriate time
- ☐ choosing a neutral place
- ☐ listening and validating
- ☐ taking responsibility
- ☐ being specific
- ☐ being positive and calm
- ☐ being firm.

What would you like to communicate?

_____

_____

Write out what you would like to say:

_____

_____

_____

_____

_____

Describe how you will communicate this message (e.g., when, where, in what mood):

_____

_____

_____

Evaluate how you did:

_____

_____

Examples of active listening

Below are examples of three techniques for active listening.

Seeking clarification
Family member 1:

> That's just what we university students do. Harmless fun. Nothing serious. So you shouldn't worry about it.

Family member 2:

> Are you saying that you don't think I should be concerned about your drug use at these parties?

Paraphrasing
Family member 1:

> I'm sick of being nagged about my drinking. You don't know how stressful my work has been. If I didn't have a drink now and then, I wouldn't be able to handle things.

Family member 2:

> You're fed up with me asking you not to drink as much. You feel a need for alcohol to help you cope with your work.

Validating
Family member 1:

> I'm so annoyed. You insist on me not going out with my buddies after work, and yet you come home late yourself.

Family member 2:

I can understand that you'd be angry with me, given that you didn't receive my message that I'd be home late from work. I also get annoyed when I'm expecting to have supper with you and you don't come home.

Family member 1:

How am I supposed to know if you're telling the truth? I have to find out for myself.

Family member 2:

It makes sense that you might have difficulty trusting me, because your previous partner frequently lied to you.

Family member 1:

I don't think I'm going to be able to go through with this. I'm freaked out about this job interview.

Family member 2:

I'd be freaked out too. It's normal to feel nervous when going to a job interview.

Practising more active listening

Indicate which of the following you are doing well:

☐ Listening attentively (stopping what you are doing, looking at the listener, demonstrating interest [e.g., nodding, verbally responding], not interrupting)

☐ Seeking clarification (not jumping to conclusions or making assumptions, but asking the speaker about his or her intended message)

☐ Paraphrasing (repeating in your own words what you have heard)

☐ Validating (stating the feelings, thoughts and behaviours of the other person that make sense to you; expressing your understanding of what the person is saying)

Select one of the above skills to work on this week:

_____

Over the next week, try to work on this listening skill during at least one of your interactions with the person in your family who has a substance use problem.

Describe the interaction:

_____

_____

Describe the response of your listener:

_____

_____

Evaluate how you did:

_____

_____

Effective speaking

The DESC framework will help you speak specifically, positively and assertively:

Describe the situation: "When you . . ." (behaviour)

Express your feelings: "I feel . . ." (emotion)

Specify what you want: "I would like / prefer . . ." (need or desire)

Communicate the consequences: "I will . . ." (positive payoff)
                                            "You will . . ." (positive payoff)

Adapted from Bower, S. & Bower, A. (2004). *Asserting Yourself: A Practical Guide for Positive Change.* Cambridge, MA: Da Capo Press.

USING THE FRAMEWORK

The following examples show how to use the DESC framework. The first example is broken down into the four parts.

D "When you leave your dishes in the sink . . .

E ". . . I feel annoyed. . . ."

S ". . . I'd like you to put them in the dishwasher. . . ."

C ". . . Then I'll have more time to spend relaxing with you in the evenings."

> When you criticize me in front of my friends, I feel embarrassed and defensive. I'd prefer that you wait until we're alone to let me know what's bothering you. Then I'll be able to listen better to you.

> When you leave drug paraphernalia lying around the house, I feel angry and alarmed. I'd prefer that you not have it in the house—or if you do, that you hide it well. If you do this, I'll be less likely to fight with you about your drug use.

> When you drink while we're out at a restaurant, I get nervous and uncomfortable. I'd like you to be sober when we go out together, so I can be more relaxed and we can enjoy the evening.

Examples of effective speaking

Below are examples of ways to expand the DESC framework for effective speaking by adding statements that are validating or that demonstrate a willingness to help. These statements are shown in **bold**.

USING THE DESC FRAMEWORK WITH VALIDATION

Given our current financial situation, when you spend so much on clothing, I feel anxious. **I have seen how good you feel about yourself when you get new clothing, so I can understand why it must be so appealing to you.** I'd prefer that you cut back on clothes shopping until we're in a better financial situation. If you do this, we'll both be less stressed about our finances and can begin to pay off our debts. Although we may feel the pinch in the short term, we'll be better off financially later on.

When you're not around in the evenings to help put the children to bed, I feel overwhelmed and stressed. **I understand how difficult it is for you to get home by 8:00 p.m., given your recent promotion and how hard you are working.** I'd prefer that you arrange to be home by the children's bedtime at least a few times a week. If you can do this, I'll be able to parent better and will feel less tired in the evenings, and I'll more fun to be with.

I feel sad when you don't plan anything special for our anniversary. **I can imagine that you might overlook our anniversaries given that your parents never celebrated theirs** but it's important to me. I'd prefer that you spontaneously remember our anniversary, which will make me feel more loved and loving toward you.

USING THE DESC FRAMEWORK WITH WILLINGNESS TO PROBLEM SOLVE

Given our current financial situation, when you spend so much on clothing, I feel anxious. **Perhaps we can look over our finances together and figure out ways to reduce our spending, so we can start paying off our debts.**

When you're not around in the evenings to help put the children to bed, I feel overwhelmed and stressed. **I'd love to sit down together with you and brainstorm possible ways of dealing with this situation so the evenings are easier for me and our children are better cared for.**

When you don't plan anything special for our anniversary, I feel hurt. I'm not sure how to help you with this, but **perhaps we could discuss the problem together and come up with a solution.**

Practising more effective speaking

Think about what you would like to communicate to your relative who has a substance use problem, and complete the following phrases using the DESC framework. Try to pick situations that do not involve too much conflict.

When you _____

I feel _____

I would prefer _____

Then I will _____

When you _____

I feel _____

I would prefer _____

Then I will _____

Plan to communicate one of these examples this week. Fill in the time and place you plan to do so below:

Time: _____   Place: _____

Remember to:
· choose an appropriate time and a neutral place
· be specific, positive, calm and firm
· listen and validate
· take responsibility.
    Describe how it went.

_____

_____

_____

Problem solving

OBJECTIVES

· to teach group members the steps of problem solving: defining problems (including brainstorming), choosing solutions and implementing solutions (including evaluating the solution that they choose)
· to empower group members to manage problems more effectively
· to provide the opportunity for group members to tackle problems in a new way

HANDOUTS

11-1: Defining Problems
11-2: Choosing Solutions
11-3: Implementing the Solution

SESSION OUTLINE

· Opening and announcements (approx. 5 min.)
· Check-in and review of last week's home practice (approx. 30 min.)
· Teaching and discussion (approx. 60 min.)
· Assigning of next week's home practice (approx. 5 min.)
· Closing (approx. 5 min.)

Teaching and discussion

DEFINING PROBLEMS

Ask the group members how they usually respond to problems.

Explain that problem-solving strategies lead to:

· an increased feeling of control and self-efficacy (the feeling that one can handle the challenges of life)

· an increased likelihood of becoming "unstuck" (use the analogy of car tires spinning on ice to illustrate how many of us become stuck when dealing with problems: we often get into the rut of doing more of the same with increased intensity, only to find that our wheels continue to spin and get us nowhere)

· an increased likelihood of solving a problem.

▶ **Distribute or turn to Handout 11-1: Defining Problems. Ask the group members to spend a few moments thinking of and writing down a problem they are experiencing in relation to their relative's substance use.**

Ask them to share the problems that they have identified with the group. Ask them how they feel about their problem.

Discuss the steps for defining problems. Read the example presented in Handout 11-1. Ask the group members to imagine being in this person's shoes and to observe how they feel after reading the general description, after reading the problem broken down into parts, and then after reading the chosen problem to work on. Explain that although the steps may seem unnecessary, they help to make problems more specific and manageable.

▶ **Ask the participants to complete the handout by breaking down their own problem into parts and then identifying the part they would like to tackle first.**

Ask them to share what they have written with the group. If any participants have not been able to break down their problem sufficiently or do not choose a manageable enough problem, have the group help them refine their answers. Ask the group members how they feel now that they have selected a specific problem to work on.

CHOOSING SOLUTIONS

▶ **Distribute or turn to Handout 11-2: Choosing Solutions.**

Discuss the steps involved in choosing solutions. Go through the example presented on Handout 11-2 with the group. Emphasize that often people have already tried many methods to deal with a problem, and that they may just need to rework one of these approaches. Explain that although difficult, it is very important to be consistent in how they handle a problem; this may be the only thing they need to do differently to solve a problem effectively, as in the example presented. Emphasize that during the brainstorming phase of developing solutions, they should write down all of their own or their relative's ideas (even ideas they do not like) and not evaluate them until the end. Advise them to consider their own safety when choosing a solution to implement. For example, if it seems that a family member might react violently if a certain solution is implemented, it might be best to seek out a different solution.

▶ **Choose one of the participants' problems and go through the steps as a group, using a blackboard, whiteboard or flipchart to record ideas.**

Then ask the participants to complete the handout themselves and share what they have written with the group.

Encourage them to go through this process again at home with their relative, using another problem or the problem they are currently tackling.

IMPLEMENTING SOLUTIONS

▶ **Distribute or turn to Handout 11-3: Implementing the Solution.**

Read over the list of steps for implementing solutions. You may do one of the following or move on to the next step:

· Ask the group members to use the example presented in this module (the person who gets too many urgent calls at work from a partner) to work through the first three steps together.

· Ask a group member to use his or her proposed solution for the group to work through the first three steps.

▶ **Ask the group members to complete the first three steps themselves.**

Then ask them to share how they intend to implement their solution during the week. Spend time considering what might interfere with implementing the solution and brainstorming about how to overcome these barriers. Consider any safety risks that might arise and discuss how to manage them.

Explain to the group members that in some cases, they may need to repeat the planned solution consistently many times before evaluating whether it has worked. Remind the participants that the problem might get worse before it gets better, because of how their relative may react to the changes. Encourage the group members to persist unless their safety or that of another person (e.g., a child) is at risk.

Home practice

Have the group members try out and evaluate a solution, using the steps outlined in Handout 11-3.

For more information

For more information on using and teaching problem-solving techniques, the following book may be helpful:

Chang, E.C., D'Zurilla, T.J. & Sanna, L.J. (Eds.) (2004). *Social Problem Solving: Theory, Research and Training*. Washington, DC: American Psychological Association.

Defining problems

Step 1: Identify a problem.
Step 2: Break down the problem into parts so that it seems less overwhelming.
Step 3: Choose which part of the problem you will target first.

EXAMPLE:

Step 1: I don't like it when I get urgent calls from my partner many times a day when I am at work, sometimes during important meetings. She calls crying and often in a crisis, and demands that I help her and even that I come home from work. Sometimes she threatens to hurt herself if I don't give in. She wants to talk for a long time when she calls, although the conversation is not helpful. Often she has been drinking when this happens. If I do not help her, she keeps phoning repeatedly. Sometimes she even calls my colleagues to get me to talk to her. Sometimes I give in just to stop the phone calls. I get embarrassed at work by the repetitive phone calls—and I am afraid that I might lose my job.

Step 2:
· receiving calls from my partner many times a day
· receiving calls from my partner during important meetings at work
· receiving calls from my partner when she has been drinking
· my partner demanding that I fix the problem
· my partner demanding that I come home
· my partner talking to me for a long time while I am at work
· my partner threatening to hurt herself
· my partner calling me repeatedly
· my partner calling my colleagues
· me giving in to my partner when she behaves like this

Step 3: I am first going to work on not accepting phone calls from my partner when she has been drinking.

Now it is your turn. Think about a problem that is related to your relative's substance use. Use the headings below to analyze the problem.

Step 1: Identify the problem.

_____

_____

_____

_____

_____

Step 2: Break down the problem into parts so that it seems less overwhelming.

_____

_____

_____

_____

_____

_____

_____

Step 3: Choose which part of the problem you will target first.

_____

_____

Choosing solutions

Step 1: Identify a specific problem to target.

Step 2: If possible, ask your relative with a substance use problem to help develop solutions.

Step 3: List approaches that have already been tried.

Step 4: Identify which of these solutions might still work if used somewhat differently (e.g., at a different time).

Step 5: Brainstorm other possible solutions without evaluating them.

Step 6: Choose a solution to try, and a back-up solution in case your first choice does not work.

Example:

PROBLEM	Accepting phone calls from my partner while I am at work when she has been drinking
SOLUTIONS ALREADY TRIED	Yelling at my partner Threatening to leave my partner Hanging up on my partner Refusing to answer the phone when she calls Leaving work, saying that I have an off-site appointment, and then going to help her Only taking her phone call when she is really in an emergency
SOLUTIONS TO REWORK	Refusing to answer the phone when she calls I could try to do this more consistently. I usually will accept the first phone call and then refuse to answer subsequent calls until I become so exasperated or embarrassed that I pick up on the 10th call or so. Sometimes I only accept calls when she seems really distressed. Perhaps I should try to determine if she has been drinking and then restrict her calls. So, if I detect that my partner has been drinking, even if she is really distressed or seems to be in an emergency, I could inform her that I will accept no more phone calls from her for the rest of the work day and remain firm in that. I will need to get call display on my phone at work, though. I could talk to my boss

(cont'd)	about acquiring a new phone. I guess I will also need to tell my co-workers about my plan, so that they do not take calls from her. I might feel better refusing her calls if I give her a list of numbers that she can call in an emergency.
OTHER POSSIBLE SOLUTIONS	I could limit all phone calls from my partner while at work. As I mentioned above, I could give her a list of emergency numbers and hotlines and tell her to call them. I could not answer phone calls from my partner in the afternoon because it is usually then that she starts drinking. I could take a break from work the first time she calls and work through her problem that time only. I could refuse to accept phone calls from my partner, but call her periodically to check on her. I could quit my job and find a job I can do from home.
CHOSEN SOLUTIONS	I will refuse any phone calls from my partner if she has been drinking, even if she is distraught, in an emergency, calling me repeatedly, or calling my colleagues. I will get call display at work so I can screen calls, and if necessary, turn off my ringer so that I and others are less bothered by the repeated calling. I will tell my colleagues never to accept phone calls from her. I will give her a list of emergency numbers that she can call when she is upset. After doing this for a month, and if I do not think it is working, I will refuse all phone calls from her while I am at work.

Now it is your turn. Use the chart below to choose a strategy for solving the problem that you identified in Handout 11-1.

PROBLEM	
SOLUTIONS ALREADY TRIED	
SOLUTIONS TO REWORK	
OTHER POSSIBLE SOLUTIONS	
CHOSEN SOLUTIONS	

Implementing the solution

Step 1: Identify the chosen solution.

Step 2: Describe the plan for implementing the solution including:

· when you will do so

· where you will do so

· how you will do so

· how you will communicate the solution to your relative with the substance use problem or to others, if appropriate

· how you will deal with possible negative reactions or barriers that may arise as you implement the solution.

Step 3: Implement the solution.

Step 4: Reward yourself for having tried the solution.

Step 5: Evaluate how well the solution worked.

Step 6: Decide on a next step:

· reworking the solution and implementing it again

· planning and trying an alternative solution

· moving on to a new problem.

Use the following chart to work out how to implement the solution that you chose in Handout 11-2.

SOLUTION TO IMPLEMENT	
PLAN INCLUDING WHEN, WHERE, HOW	
REWARD	
EVALUATION	
NEXT STEPS	

Setting goals and making change happen

OBJECTIVES

· to help group members develop a positive vision for their lives, focusing not on their current situation but on what they would like to have happen
· to instruct group members about ways of setting and achieving goals
· to facilitate change among group members by helping them identify goals, break down these goals into steps, and implement the steps

HANDOUTS

12-1: The Miracle Question
12-2: Creating a Vision
12-3: Defining Problems and Setting Goals
12-4: Examples of Goals
12-5: Implementing Goals
12-6: Achieving My Goal

SESSION OUTLINE

· Opening and announcements (approx. 5 min.)
· Check-in and review of last week's home practice (approx. 30 min.)
· Teaching and discussion (approx. 60 min.)
· Assigning of next week's home practice (approx. 5 min.)
· Closing (approx. 5 min.)

Teaching and discussion

NOTE: If time is limited, you may want to go directly to "Setting Goals" (page 226) because the section "Thinking Positively about the Future" requires a fair amount of time to do well. Alternatively, you may divide this module over two weeks, covering "Thinking Positively about the Future" in the first week and "Setting Goals" and "Achieving Goals" in the second week.

THINKING POSITIVELY ABOUT THE FUTURE

In this module, we provide two options to help group members think positively about the future:

· an exercise taken from solution-focused therapy, called the Miracle Question
· a similar exercise that we have developed, entitled Creating a Vision.

While the Miracle Question is very effective, Creating a Vision is more straightforward and thus easier to explain and use, particularly when facilitating a group. We recommend that you use Creating a Vision if you are not experienced in facilitating the Miracle Question, and/or you have a large group and so may not be able to give individual help to people struggling with the concept of the Miracle Question.

Option 1: The Miracle Question

▶ **Distribute or turn to Handout 12-1: The Miracle Question. Ask the group members to complete the handout.**

Emphasize that they should be specific about their feelings, thoughts and actions as they describe the "miracle." Encourage the group members not to focus on how the person with a substance use problem would behave, but rather on how they themselves would think, feel and act. Encourage them not to get bogged down by skepticism or pessimism, but to give their imaginations free rein. Remind them that they are imagining a miracle, and thus anything could happen.

Ask the group members to present their miracle to the group.

Help them to change vague statements about their miracle into specific behavioural statements. If they are focusing on their relative's behaviour, help them instead to imagine how they themselves would behave or relate to that person.

Ask the participants what part of the miracle they are already doing. Instruct them to place a star next to these sections of their miracle. Ask them then what they can start doing right now to implement their miracle. Tell them to underline one part of the miracle they can begin to implement.

FOR MORE INFORMATION

For more information on implementing the Miracle Question, see:

Metcalfe, L. (1998). *Solution Focused Group Therapy*. New York: Free Press.

Metcalfe, L. (2007). *The Miracle Question: Answer It and Change Your Life*. Norwalk, CT: Crown House Publishing.

Santa Rita, E.L. (1998). What do you do after asking the miracle question in solution-focused therapy? *Family Therapy, 25* (1), 189–195.

Option 2: Creating a vision

▶ **Distribute or turn to Handout 12-2: Creating a Vision. Ask the group members to spend about five minutes completing the handout.**

Ask the group members to spend a few moments imagining the life that they would like to have in the near future. Ask them to imagine what they would like to be doing, thinking and feeling, and how they would be relating to others, in a year from now. Encourage them to emphasize their own actions, thoughts and feelings, not those of the person with a substance use problem. Encourage them not to get bogged down by skepticism or pessimism, but to be optimistic (and even perhaps unrealistic) about what might be possible.

Ask the participants to present part of their vision to the group. Help them to change vague statements about their vision into specific behavioural statements. If they are focusing on their relative's behaviour, help them instead to imagine how they themselves would behave or relate to that person in the future.

Ask the group members to indicate what part of the vision they are already achieving. Instruct them to place a star next to these sections of their vision. Ask them what parts of this vision they can begin implementing now. Tell them to underline one section of the vision that they can begin to implement.

Advise group members of the importance of keeping their eyes fixed on this vision as they set goals and of tackling small parts of this vision every day.

SETTING GOALS

▶ **Distribute or turn to Handout 12-3: Defining Problems and Setting Goals, and Handout 12-4: Examples of Goals.**

Talk about goal setting. Goals should be specific, detailed and behavioural. Read through some of the examples of general and specific goals listed on Handout 12-4.

▶ **Ask the group members to write down on Handout 12-3 at least two specific problems they are having and two related goals they would like to attain.**

Ask them to share one of these problems and the related goal with the group. You may need to help the participants formulate appropriate goals:

· If goals are not specific, detailed and behavioural, help the group members reformulate their goals.
· If goals are focused on or dependent on the behavioural change of the person who has a substance use problem, suggest that the group members develop more personal goals.
· If goals are potentially unattainable (e.g., they are too long term), help the group members to set shorter-term, attainable goals.

ACHIEVING GOALS

Ask the group members what has helped them attain goals in the past.

▶ **Write down their answers on a blackboard, whiteboard or flipchart.**

Then distribute or turn to Handout 12-5: Implementing Goals.

Explain each step in the left column. Ask group members to volunteer to read the examples in the right column.

▶ **Distribute or turn to Handout 12-6: Achieving My Goal.**

Ask a group member to volunteer to use his or her problem statement and goal, and to work through all the steps from defining the problem to the end.
Ask the group members to choose one of their goals and to begin working on Handout 12-6 on their own. Ask them to share with the group their goal and how they will achieve it. Solicit feedback from the other group members regarding their plans.

Home practice

Ask the group members to complete Handout 12-6: Achieving My Goal.

The Miracle Question

After thinking about your personal situation, take a few moments to think about, and then to answer, the following question:

Suppose one night, while you were asleep, there was a miracle and the issues that brought you to this group were resolved. When you woke up:

· how would you know that anything had changed?

· how would you be thinking, feeling and acting?

· what would you be doing differently?

Provide as much detail as you need to describe what your life would be like after this "miracle."

_____

_____

_____

_____

_____

_____

_____

_____

_____

_____

_____

_____

_____

_____

_____

_____

_____

_____

_____

_____

_____

Creating a vision

Take a few moments to develop a vision of what you would like your life to look like in a year. Be as specific as possible. Focus on your behaviour, not that of the person in your life who has a substance use problem.

Here are some questions that may help you create your vision:

· What would you be thinking?
· What would you be feeling?
· What would you be doing?
· What would you be accomplishing?
· What would you be focusing on?
· How would you be spending your time?
· How would you be relating to others?
· How would you be responding to others?
· How would you be dealing with problems?
· What would your priorities be?
· What would your goals be?

_____

_____

_____

_____

_____

_____

_____

_____

_____

_____

_____

_____

_____

_____

_____

_____

_____

Defining problems and setting goals

Problems are most easily tackled when they are *specific* and *broken down into parts*.

Goals are most helpful and attainable when they are based on a well-defined problem, and when they are specific, detailed and behavioural.

Choose at least two problems related to the person in your life who has a substance use problem. In the first column of the chart, describe each problem. In the second column, describe one or more specific, detailed goals related to the problem.

PROBLEMS	GOALS

Examples of goals

GENERAL GOALS	SPECIFIC GOALS
I want to be less stressed.	I will use breathing techniques to reduce my anxiety when coming home from work in the evening.
	I will take a yoga (or other exercise) class once a week at the local gym.
	I will attend a weekly support group for partners or family members affected by substance use.
I want my marriage and family life to be more fulfilling.	I will arrange to have a babysitter look after the children every Monday evening so that my partner and I can go out for dinner.
	I will refrain from yelling at my partner when he/she comes home drunk, and instead will briefly tell him/her how I feel, leave the conversation until he/she is sober, and in the meantime do something for myself.
	I will demonstrate understanding for my partner's situation and feelings when discussing problems.
I want to help my relative stop drinking or using other substances.	I will stop covering up for my relative when he/she misses work because of substance use, so that he/she experiences the consequences of his/her substance use.
	I will attend a therapy group designed to help me deal more effectively with the person who has a substance use problem.
	I will support my relative's recovery by telling him/her how much I value the work that he/she is doing and how much it is helping our relationship.
I want to become a better parent.	I will schedule 15 minutes every day to spend directly with each of my children.
	I will arrange to attend half of my child's soccer games.

(cont'd)	I will talk to my children about their mother's/father's substance use and reassure them that they are not to blame.
I want to feel less depressed.	I will set the alarm for 7:00 a.m. and get out of bed when it rings, regardless of how I feel.
	I will phone my friend and suggest that we regularly go out for dinner on Friday evenings.
	I will enrol in a weekly dance class in my neighbourhood.

Implementing goals

Ways to increase the likelihood of being able to achieve goals:

STEPS	EXAMPLES
1. Define the problem.	I am feeling isolated and alone and lack support in dealing with my relative's substance use.
2. Set a specific, achievable goal.	I will seek support for myself by telling my sister about my relative's substance use problem.
3. Break down the goal into steps.	I will ask my sister out for dinner. I will explain to my sister that I need her to listen without judging me. I will tell her the extent of my relative's problem.
4. Plan when you will achieve the goal.	I will ask if my sister is free this Saturday or Sunday evening at 6:00 p.m. (I do not want to wait too long because the wait may increase my anxiety and make me lose my nerve).
5. Look for ways to make the process easier or more enjoyable.	I will choose my favourite restaurant.
6. Tell someone your goal.	I will tell my family support and education group about my goal to get the support of my sister.
7. Troubleshoot about anything that will get in the way.	I will remind myself that my relative's drinking is not my fault and not a reflection of me, and that I am trying to take positive steps for my family and me. I will remember that the best way to reduce unwarranted shame is to disclose my "shameful secret."
8. Rehearse the steps and visualize yourself achieving the goal.	I will write down what I plan to say and then practise it aloud in front of the mirror until I feel more comfortable.

9. Say encouraging things to yourself as you make plans and take steps toward your goal.	"I can do this." "I believe that my sister and I can once again have a close relationship. I think that my sister will be pleased to be invited out to supper and to be brought into my confidence." "I am a good family member / partner."
10. Reward yourself for every step that you take.	Verbal rewards: "Good job"; "I did it." Time rewards: read for 15 minutes, go for a 30-minute bike ride Tangible rewards: dessert, money toward trip

Achieving my goal

Take one of the problems you identified in Handout 12-3 and develop a strategy for achieving the goal you set, by following the steps outlined below.

1. Define the problem.

_____

_____

_____

2. Set a specific, achievable goal.

_____

_____

_____

3. Break down the goal into steps.

_____

_____

_____

_____

4. Plan when you will achieve the goal.

_____

_____

_____

5. Look for ways to make the process easier or more enjoyable.

_____

_____

6. Tell someone your goal.

_____

_____

7. Troubleshoot about anything that will get in the way.

_____

_____

_____

_____

_____

8. Rehearse the steps and visualize yourself achieving the goal.

_____

_____

9. Say encouraging things to yourself as you make plans and take steps toward your goal.

_____

_____

_____

10. Reward yourself for every step that you take.

_____

_____

_____

PROGRESSING TOWARD MY GOAL

As you put your strategy into action, keep a record of your experiences by filling in the information below.

Steps that I took this week toward my goal:

_____

_____

Problems that I encountered in taking these steps:

_____

_____

Problem solving that I engaged in to eliminate these problems:

_____

_____

Rewards I received (from myself, from others or from the situation itself) from taking these steps:

_____

_____

Steps I intend to take next:

_____

_____

Responding to a person who has a substance use problem

OBJECTIVES

· to provide a supportive environment in which group members can explore their own helpful and unhelpful responses to their relative's substance use
· to help group members with the consequences of their responses, both for themselves and for their relative
· to provide group members with more helpful ways of responding to the person who has a substance use problem

HANDOUTS

13-1: Less Helpful Ways of Responding to a Person Who Has a Substance Use Problem

13-2: More Helpful Ways of Responding to a Person Who Has a Substance Use Problem

13-3: Practising More Helpful Ways of Responding

SESSION OUTLINE

· Opening and announcements (approx. 5 min.)
· Check-in and review of last week's home practice (approx. 30 min.)
· Teaching and discussion (approx. 60 min.)
· Assigning of next week's home practice (approx. 5 min.)
· Closing (approx. 5 min.)

Teaching and discussion

Ask the group members to share what they have tried to do to help or deal with the person who has a substance use problem. Do not criticize any ways of responding. Instead, emphasize that they have been coping the best that they can in their situation, and that their responses, even if unhealthy or unhelpful, are common. In fact, some such responses would actually be healthy and helpful within more healthy family relationships.

▶ **Distribute or turn to Handout 13-1: Less Helpful Ways of Responding to a Person Who Has a Substance Use Problem.**

Describe each category of ways of helping, and read through the examples. Ask the group members to give other examples for each category. Some of these responses (e.g., those in the "protecting" category) are actually very loving and would be helpful in most normal or healthy relationships. It is because of the substance use problem that they become unhelpful.

CONSEQUENCES

▶ **Ask the group members to write down on Handout 13-1 what they think are the consequences of each of these ways of responding, for themselves, for the person with a substance use problem, and for the rest of the family. Encourage them to think of as many consequences as possible.**

If some of the consequences below are not mentioned, you may add them.

Family members may notice the following consequences for themselves:
· increased stress and distress
· increased anger and resentment
· increased preoccupation with the relative's problems
· increased engagement in a vicious cycle that worsens both parties' unhelpful responses (e.g., person trying to help nags → person with substance use problem lies → temporary reinforcement of nagging and lying → increased nagging from person trying to help → increased lying . . .)
· increased feeling of helplessness
· decreased safety (e.g., controlling behaviours can result in a person with a substance use problem becoming angry and even violent)
· decreased integrity (as the person responds in ways that he or she does not like)
· decreased ability to respect their own and others' boundaries
· decreased focus on self and self-care

· decreased energy for other relationships
· less functional relationship.

    The person who has a substance use problem may experience the following consequences:

· increased tendency to be secretive and to lie
· increased feeling of resentment, anger and annoyance
· increased likelihood of tuning out the other person
· decreased likelihood of facing and dealing with the consequences of substance use
· decreased likelihood of making lasting changes
· less functional relationship.

▶ **Discuss the advantages for family members themselves of responding in more healthy and helpful ways. Write these on a blackboard, whiteboard or flipchart.**

    For example, by reducing the unhealthy ways of responding, group members are likely to find they have:

· increased integrity
· better and healthier boundaries
· less stress and distress
· greater self-care
· more energy for other relationships.

    They will also be more likely to have a supportive influence on the behaviour and recovery of the person with a substance use problem. Stress that group members are not responsible for changing the other person, but that reducing unhelpful responses will increase their own quality of life, will improve the relationship, and may result in helping the other person to recover.

RESPONDING IN MORE HELPFUL WAYS

▶ **Distribute or turn to Handout 13-2: More Helpful Ways of Responding to a Person Who Has a Substance Use Problem.**

Talk about alternative ways of responding. Ask the group members to give examples of situations in which they have used each of these alternative approaches. Ask about the effects of these approaches on themselves and on the person with a substance use problem.

▶ **Distribute or turn to Handout 13-3: Practising More Helpful Ways of Responding. Ask the participants to complete the first two questions and to tell the group what response strategy they will try to use this week.**

BARRIERS TO RESPONDING IN MORE HELPFUL WAYS

Ask the group members what prevents them from responding in more helpful ways to the person who has a substance use problem.

▶ **Write the responses on a blackboard, whiteboard or flipchart.**

Validate the difficulty of changing how we respond in relationships. Take seriously group members' struggles and concerns regarding trying new methods of change. You may encounter participants who say they have tried some of the more helpful approaches without success. You can respond by saying that not every approach will work in every situation, and encourage them to try another approach. You can also investigate how the response was used. Healthy responses often do not work because they are not used appropriately or consistently.

Warn group members that they may not get a positive response from their relative, particularly if they choose to reduce the amount of protecting and fixing. The other person's initial response may be anger and possibly even aggression, particularly when a group member first changes the way he or she responds. Group members need to weigh the short-term and long-term benefits of responding in different ways.

Caution group members to consider any safety risks to themselves or others when they try new ways of responding. State that although you recommend that they avoid unhelpful ways of responding, there may be times when they choose to continue using them because of safety issues. Stress, however, that they should do so only temporarily and should explore means of increasing their safety, such as setting and enforcing limits, restricting contact, calling the police, leaving the relationship or, if necessary, finding a safe house.

You might want to discuss with participants that there may be ways in which they choose to protect the person who has a substance use problem (e.g., by picking up the person from a bar when he or she is drunk, or giving the person money so he or she does not become homeless). Tell them them that everyone has to make his or her own decisions about these situations, but that it is important to remember that any form of protecting decreases the extent to which the person has to face and deal with the negative consequences of his or her substance use. Remind the group members that one of the most effective ways of helping a person become more motivated to change is to allow the person to experience the negative consequences of his or her substance use.

Home practice

Complete Handout 13-3 by actually practising new responses and documenting how this went.

Less helpful ways of responding to a person who has a substance use problem

How you respond to the person who has a substance use problem affects you and your well-being, as well as the well-being of your relative and other family members.

Think about possible consequences to the types of responses listed in the first column in the chart. Write your answers in the second column.

LESS HELPFUL RESPONSES	CONSEQUENCES
NAGGING Lecturing the person about his or her behaviour Frequently asking the person to stop using substances Reminding the person of the consequences of his or her behaviour Pleading with the person to change	
CONTROLLING Hiding drugs Setting up treatment for the person Pouring alcohol down the sink Hiding the person's wallet or keys Not passing on messages to the person from substance-using associates or dealers	
INVESTIGATING Searching the house Making phone calls to locate the person Calling the treatment facility to determine if the person is attending appointments Frequently questioning the person Being preoccupied with the person's behaviour	

Following the person Listening to or tracing calls made by the person	
FIXING Apologizing for the person's behaviour to children, friends or family Cleaning up after the person Paying the person's debt Nursing the person's substance use–related injuries Cutting back on your own spending to deal with reduced finances	
PROTECTING Covering up for the person to protect the person from losing his or her job Picking up the person after a drinking binge Waking the person so he or she can get to work Minimizing the seriousness of the person's behaviour Consoling the person when he or she expresses guilt or shame over substance use	

More helpful ways of responding to a person who has a substance use problem

How you respond to the person who has a substance use problem affects you and your well-being, as well as that of the other person and other family members.

INSTEAD OF	ALTERNATIVE MORE HELPFUL RESPONSES
NAGGING	Speak to the person using the DESC model,* when neither of you is upset or drinking alcohol or using other drugs:
	Describe the situation: "When you . . ." (behaviour)
	Express your feelings: "I feel . . ." (emotion)
	Specify what you want: "I would like . . ." (need/ desire)
	Communicate the consequences: "I will . . ." (positive payoff) "You will . . ." (positive payoff) "If . . . then . . ." (negative consequences should the behaviour not change)
	Be clear about what you will and will not tolerate—in other words, what your limits are.
CONTROLLING	Identify what you are and are not responsible for.
	Focus on changing your own behaviour (e.g., how you communicate, how you respond, how you handle conflict).
	Accept what you cannot change.
	Reinforce the person when he or she does not drink alcohol or use other substances (e.g., by having a nice dinner together, watching a movie together).
	Withdraw attention whenever the person is using substances (e.g., leave the room, situation, apartment).
	Suggest activities that you can do with the person that do not involve substance use and that are enjoyable to both of you (e.g., playing tennis, going for a hike).
	Ask the person how you can help him or her in his or her recovery.

INVESTIGATING	Tell the person how you feel when he or she is not honest or reliable ("I feel disappointed/confused/anxious . . .").
	Communicate and follow through on limits.
	Allow the person to take responsibility for his or her own recovery.
	Focus on other aspects of your life.
FIXING	Allow the person to be responsible for his or her own behaviour and choices.
	Allow the person to fix his or her own messes.
PROTECTING	Allow the person to experience the consequences of his or her behaviour and choices.
	Remember, you are not responsible for changing the person who has a substance use problem, but by reducing the number of unhelpful responses and increasing the more helpful ones, you will improve the quality of your own life and your relationship with the person, and you may help the other person move toward recovery.

* Bower, S. & Bower, A. (2004). *Asserting Yourself: A Practical Guide for Positive Change.* Cambridge, MA: Da Capo Press.

Practising more helpful ways of responding

Describe a response that you give that may not be helpful.

_____

_____

Describe an alternative way of responding that might be more helpful.

_____

_____

Practise responding this way on at least two occasions during the week. Use the chart to describe the situation, your response and the consequences.

SITUATION	RESPONSE	CONSEQUENCES OF YOUR RESPONSE
Example: My son asks me to drive him to work because he has a hangover.	I tell him politely yet firmly that I will not drive him to work.	My son yelled and swore at me, and threatened that he would not then go to work and would likely lose his job. I felt angry and scared. I questioned my decision and worried that he would lose his job. I did not give in. I left the house. I later found out that he did eventually go to work, albeit four hours late, and that he took a taxi. I felt proud that I did not give in, did not feel resentful and did not get into a fight with him.

SITUATION	RESPONSE	CONSEQUENCES OF YOUR RESPONSE

SITUATION	RESPONSE	CONSEQUENCES OF YOUR RESPONSE

Supporting the recovery of a person with a substance use problem

OBJECTIVES

- to help group members develop realistic expectations about recovery
- to help group members cope better with the recovery process
- to validate the difficulties experienced by group members in supporting the recovery of person who has a substance use problem
- to provide suggestions about how group members might support the recovery of a relative with a substance use problem
- to help group members develop a greater understanding of their own recovery

HANDOUTS

14-1: Recovery, Relapse and Relapse Prevention
14-2: Coping with Recovery
14-3: Stages of Change
14-4: Goals and Tasks of Each Stage of Change
14-5: Letting Go
14-6: Ways of Supporting Recovery
14-7: Supporting Recovery

· Opening and announcements (approx. 5 min.)
· Check-in and review of last week's home practice (approx. 30 min.)
· Teaching and discussion (approx. 60 min.)
· Assigning of next week's home practice (approx. 5 min.)
· Closing (approx. 5 min.)

NOTE: This is another very full module and could be divided into two sessions. If you do so, we recommend that the first session deal with learning about treatment and recovery, the effects of recovery on families, and how they can cope with this process. This session would include Handouts 14-1 and 14-2. The second session should deal with learning about the stages of change and how to support recovery within this model. This session would include Handouts 14-3 to 14-8.

Part 1: About recovery

TEACHING AND DISCUSSION

Ask the group members to share briefly about the treatment and recovery experiences of the person in their family who has a substance use problem.

▶ **Distribute or turn to Handout 14-1: Recovery, Relapse and Relapse Prevention.**

Stress that recovery is a unique, slow, exhausting and up-and-down process. Help the group members to develop realistic expectations about recovery.

Give group members the opportunity to ask questions about recovery and treatment. Be prepared to discuss:
· the pros and cons of harm reduction versus abstinence approaches to treatment
· what harm reduction is (describe the wide range of harm reduction approaches)
· the importance of family members and the person with a substance use problem not overreacting to lapses (e.g., concluding that all progress has been lost or the person has failed)
· what treatment works.

We know from research that treatment is most effective when it:
· matches the person's stage of change (discussed in part 2 of this module) and goals
· extends over a long period (e.g., six months or more) or provides long-term follow-up
· involves outpatient treatment for at least part of the program (e.g., if a residential program, it should provide outpatient follow-up care)

· treats concurrent mental health problems
· involves the family in treatment
· deals with the person's physical, social, emotional, cognitive and spiritual well-being
· includes relapse prevention training (a cognitive-behavioural approach).

The challenge of recovery for family members

Ask the group members to share more of their experiences of their relative's recovery. Discuss the challenges faced by family members during the recovery process. For example, as a person recovers from a substance use problem, family members might:
· feel that the person is emotionally unavailable
· observe the person having more difficulties in coping
· dislike the slow pace or focus of recovery
· feel as if they are on a roller coaster
· feel as if they are walking on eggshells
· feel as if they are in the dark
· feel discouraged, angry and hopeless
· receive little support or treatment themselves
· need to change their ways of relating to the person.

Coping with challenges

Discuss how group members can cope with these challenges. For example, they might:
· educate themselves about recovery
· ask the person with a substance use problem how they can help or support his or her recovery
· ask if they can be involved in the person's treatment
· work on improving how they relate to the person
· work on acknowledging and controlling their own emotions so that they are less affected by the other person's emotions
· develop realistic expectations about recovery
· get emotional support from other family members, from friends or from professionals
· join a support group
· read a related self-help book
· take care of their own needs
· take a holiday
· get treatment themselves.

HOME PRACTICE

Ask the group members to complete Handout 14-2: Coping with Recovery.

Part 2: The stages of change

TEACHING AND DISCUSSION

▶ **Distribute or turn to Handout 14-3: Stages of Change, and Handout 14-4: Goals and Tasks of Each Stage of Change.**

Explain the stages of change by using the above handouts.

Ask each person to think of a personal behaviour and identify which stage he or she is in with regard to that behaviour. Allocate a section of the room to each stage of change.

▶ **Ask that group members move to the appropriate place in the room. Once they are in these locations, ask each group what their feelings, thoughts and behaviours are about being in that stage.**

Write down their responses on chart paper in each section of the room.

Ask the participants to share what they think would help them to move to the next stage with regard to the behaviour they chose.

Stages of change and the family

Ask the group members to identify which stage their relative is in with regard to his or her substance use. Ask them to determine which stage they are in themselves with regard to their response to the other person. Discuss what happens when two people are at different stages with regard to a shared problem.

Supporting recovery

▶ **Distribute or turn to Handout 14-5: Letting Go. Ask a group member to read the Seven Cs and the Serenity Prayer aloud.**

Explain that group members are not responsible for the recovery of the person who has a substance use problem. Emphasize that while there are things they can do, there are other things beyond their control. Tell them that some family members find the Seven Cs or the Serenity Prayer help them as they try to let go of control. Encourage them to accept their lack of control. Discuss how they have managed to do this so far. Encourage them to remember these messages as they continue this session.

NOTE: The Serenity Prayer is often associated with Alcoholics Anonymous, and for some people it may be associated with the Christian faith. If clients are uncomfortable with this prayer, you may wish to forgo its use, or to encourage participants to focus on its message rather than its origin.

▶ Distribute or turn to Handout 14-6: Ways of Supporting Recovery.

Talk about how to support the person who has a substance use problem at each stage of change. Ask the group members if they have tried any of the suggestions and, if so, what the response has been.

▶ Distribute or turn to Handout 14-7: Supporting Recovery. Ask the group members to complete the first three questions in each section.

HOME PRACTICE

Ask the group members to complete Handout 14-7 in the coming week.

Recovery, relapse and relapse prevention

RECOVERY

Recovery from substance use problems:
- is a process that is unique to everyone
- involves someone making positive changes to his or her physical, mental, emotional, familial, social and/or spiritual life
- can involve a goal of abstinence or of reduced or controlled use
- can occur even when a person continues to use alcohol or other drugs
- takes time
- proceeds with many ups and downs
- can involve many lapses and relapses
- often uncovers other problems
- often requires treatment of co-occurring mental health problems
- involves learning new ways of coping and behaving
- may mean that a person needs to acquire new friends and social activities.

LAPSES AND RELAPSES

Lapses (temporary slips) or relapses (a return to problematic substance use) occur most often when a person is triggered by:
- negative emotions
- social pressures
- interpersonal problems.

Lapses may also occur due to physical urges, places or people associated with substance use, boredom, stress, pleasant emotions, celebrations or receiving money.

RELAPSE PREVENTION

Relapse prevention includes helping the person with a substance use problem to:
- recognize his or her patterns of use
- recognize triggers
- avoid high-risk situations

· remove items that might trigger substance use (e.g., alcohol in house, corkscrews)
· develop ways to resist urges (e.g., leaving the situation, distraction)
· learn new ways of dealing with triggers (e.g., with difficult emotions)
· remind himself or herself of the negative consequences of substance use
· obtain medical or psychological treatment for concurrent substance use and mental health problems
· avoid all-or-nothing thinking with regard to recovery (e.g., seeing a slip as a complete failure)
· accept that lapses will occur and to view them as opportunities for learning
· avoid overreacting to lapses (e.g., "I am a failure," "I can never recover")
· reduce feelings of shame and guilt
· set short-term, attainable goals, but to stay focused on long-term goals and ambitions (e.g., education)
· avoid attributing a relapse to unchangeable factors (e.g., "I am a failure," "I can never recover," "I am stupid," "I will never get an education").

Coping with recovery

RELAPSE PREVENTION

List challenges you are experiencing as a result of your relative's recovery:

_____

_____

_____

_____

List how you have been coping with the person's recovery:

_____

_____

_____

_____

Choose two ways to improve how you cope with the person's recovery.
Try these out this week.

1. _____

_____

_____

2. _____

_____

_____

Record how you did in coping with the person's recovery this week.

_____

_____

_____

Stages of change

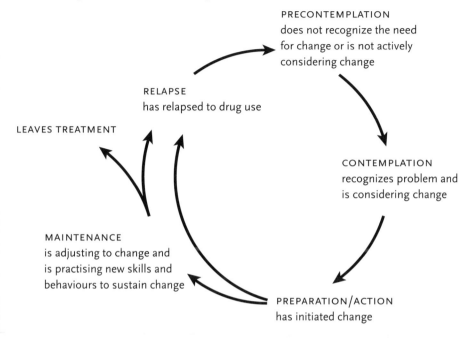

PRECONTEMPLATION
does not recognize the need
for change or is not actively
considering change

RELAPSE
has relapsed to drug use

LEAVES TREATMENT

CONTEMPLATION
recognizes problem and
is considering change

MAINTENANCE
is adjusting to change and
is practising new skills and
behaviours to sustain change

PREPARATION/ACTION
has initiated change

Source: Prochaska, J., Norcross, J. & DiClemente, C. (1995). *Changing for Good: A Revolutionary Six-Stage Program for Overcoming Bad Habits and Moving Your Life Positively Forward*. New York: Avon Books.

Goals and tasks of each stage of change

STAGE OF CHANGE	DESCRIPTION	GOALS AND TASKS
Precontemplation	Lack of awareness of the problem No interest in quitting or reducing substance use Rationalization of substance use "I have no problem."	Goal: to increase awareness and to move to the contemplation stage Task: to acknowledge the existence of a problem
Contemplation	Awareness of the problem Ambivalence about continuing versus reducing or quitting Thoughts about quitting or reducing sometime "I don't know what I will do about this problem."	Goal: to move from ambivalence to commitment Tasks: · to weigh the pros and cons of the substance use · to consider how the substance use affects goals · to realize the need for change
Preparation	Making plans to change in the near future Requesting advice and information Creating a plan	Goal: to make an action plan Tasks: · to learn about recovery · to figure out what needs to change · to develop goals, steps and timelines

STAGE OF CHANGE	DESCRIPTION	GOALS AND TASKS
Action	Taking action on plan Motivated and excited about plan Making small changes Resisting lapses and relapses Getting back on track after a lapse	Goal: to stick with action plan or modify it if necessary Tasks: · to take steps toward goals · to prevent relapses and deal with lapses · to learn about triggers · to resist urges · to develop new ways of behaving and coping · to view lapses as opportunities for learning · to get back on track quickly after lapses
Maintenance	Continuing the plan Working at establishing new patterns Engaging in relapse prevention	Goal: to maintain changes and to get back on track quickly after any lapses Tasks: · to continue to do what works · to prevent relapses and deal with lapses

Letting go

The Seven Cs

I didn't *cause* it.
I can't *cure* it.
I can't *control* it.
I can take *care* of myself.
I can *communicate* my feelings.
I can make healthy *choices*.
I can *celebrate* being me.

Source: National Association for Children of Alcoholics (NACoA)

The Serenity Prayer

> God, grant me the serenity to accept the things I cannot change, the courage to change the things I can, and the wisdom to know the difference.
>
> —Reinhold Niebuhr

Ways of supporting recovery

You are not responsible for the recovery of the person in your family who has a substance use problem.

Your first priority, regardless of what stage of change this person is in, is to:

· take care of yourself (and your children)
· get support
· focus on your own needs and recovery.

However, it can be helpful to understand where your relative is with regard to the stages of change, and how you might support him or her at different stages.

STAGE OF CHANGE	WAYS OF SUPPORTING RECOVERY
Precontemplation	Focus on raising awareness
	Educate yourself about substance use, treatment and recovery
	Provide information about the consequences of substance use in a non-threatening way
	Allow the person to experience the consequences of his or her substance use
	Be careful not to reinforce or facilitate the person's substance use
	Avoid nagging, investigating, controlling, fixing and protecting
Contemplation	Support the person as he or she weighs the pros and cons of substance use
	Support the person as he or she considers the role or impact of substance use on his or her future goals and on your future goals
	Encourage the person to learn from people who are in recovery
	Help acquire information about substance use problems and treatment
	Allow the person to experience the consequences of his or her substance use
	Be careful not to reinforce or facilitate the person's substance use
	Avoid nagging, investigating, controlling, fixing and protecting
	Avoid pushing the person toward preparation for change before he or she is ready

Preparation	Support the person in developing realistic expectations and goals
	Support the person in considering what will need to change
	Support the person in getting the help that he or she needs
	Support the person as he or she makes a plan
	Avoid pushing the person into action too quickly
	Avoid doing the "preparing" for the person
Action	Celebrate and reinforce small steps
	Support the person as he or she learns new ways of meeting needs without problematic substance use
	Support the person in avoiding or dealing with high-risk situations
	Focus on making changes in your relationship with the person, and in the family, that will support healthier living
	Be realistic about the speed of recovery
	Help remove problems that may have sustained the person's substance use
	Avoid engaging in all-or-nothing thinking
	Avoid viewing lapses as failures or as the loss of past gains. Instead, view them as opportunities for the person to learn from
	Avoid investigating and controlling the person's recovery
Maintenance	Celebrate and reinforce healthy behaviour
	Celebrate and reinforce progress toward goals
	Focus on maintaining changes in your relationship with the person, and in the family, that support healthy living
	Focus on maintaining your own recovery

Supporting recovery

Your recovery

Identify a behaviour you would like to change:

_____

Which stage are you in with regard to this behaviour?

_____

What approach might be helpful and might move you toward the next stage?

_____

_____

How did it go this week?

_____

_____

Your family member's recovery

Identify a behaviour you would like the person with a substance use problem to change:

_____

_____

Which stage is the person in with regard to this behaviour?

_____

What approach might support the person and his or her movement toward the next stage?

_____

_____

How did it go this week?

_____

Setting limits with a person who has a substance use problem

OBJECTIVES

· to help group members understand boundaries and their importance
· to facilitate group members' discovery of their own limits
· to instruct group members how to communicate limits effectively, and to provide examples
· to help group members identify and reduce barriers to their setting and enforcing limits

HANDOUTS

15-1: Boundaries and Limits
15-2: Determining My Boundaries
15-3: Barriers to Protecting Common Boundaries
15-4: Communicating Loving Limits
15-5: Communicating Limits Using the DESC Model
15-6: Setting Loving Limits

· Opening and announcements (approx. 5 min.)
· Check-in and review of last week's home practice (approx. 30 min.)
· Teaching and discussion (approx. 60 min.)
· Assigning of next week's home practice (approx. 5 min.)
· Closing (approx. 5 min.)

Teaching and discussion

NOTE: Module 15 covers a lot of material (particularly if you have not already completed Module 10: Communicating Effectively with a Person Who Has a Substance Use Problem) and if possible should be covered over two sessions or an extended session.

WHAT IS A BOUNDARY?

Ask the group members to state what is meant by a personal boundary, or how they would define the term. Here are some possible definitions:
· the shield we put around ourselves
· where one person stops and the other begins
· one's physical, emotional, sexual and social safety zones.
   Use one of the following analogies or exercises to discuss boundaries:
· Ask the group members what the purpose of clothing is (i.e., what function it plays). In essence, clothing protects us not only physically (e.g., from cold, from damage due to sun) but also emotionally (e.g., preventing other people from coming too close without permission). Clothing is a sign to others that we have boundaries and that we are protecting ourselves. We cover our bodies more extensively when we are more vulnerable and in need of more protection (e.g., in the winter, with strangers).
· If the group is not already in a circle, ask them to form one. Direct one participant to stand in the middle of the circle. Direct another group member to move toward the person in the middle. Ask the participant in the middle to say "stop" when the other person's closeness makes him or her feel uncomfortable. Ask that person if he or she would have a different boundary for a child, partner, parent, pet, neighbour, colleague or stranger. Discuss what happens when a person invades a boundary or intrudes on our space.
· Ask the group members what a door represents. Ask them when we close doors, and for what reasons. Ask them why we close the door during the group meetings.

Doors are a means of keeping people in or out, either literally or figuratively. Doors can be a form of protection. When we need privacy, we close doors. When we feel vulnerable, we may lock or double-lock them. On the other hand, when we feel safe and friendly, we open doors to allow people in.

WHY DO WE HAVE BOUNDARIES?

Discuss why we have boundaries in our relationships. Encourage the group members to generate their own answers.

▶ **Distribute or turn to Handout 15-1: Boundaries and Limits. Discuss each point of "PROTECT" together.**

You may want to discuss how maintaining boundaries and setting limits can help not only us, but also those around us, by ensuring that we don't burn out or become resentful, by modelling appropriate boundaries, by helping people learn to respect others' boundaries and limits, and by encouraging greater self-sufficiency.

Ask the group members how they protect their boundaries. Protecting boundaries involves:
· being aware of your feelings and needs
· knowing your boundaries
· setting limits on others' behaviour with respect to your boundaries
· informing others of these limits and asking that they respect them
· ensuring that others do respect your boundaries.

Refer again to Handout 15-1. Read each point of "STOP" together.

Healthy people protect boundaries and set limits in healthy relationships. Tell the group members that it is particularly important to take the initiative in maintaining their own boundaries and setting limits in their relationship with the person in their lives who has a substance use problem. People with substance use problems often take advantage of and violate others' boundaries when they are focused on acquiring and using the substance.

DETERMINING LIMITS

Ask the group members for examples of limits they have set in the past in their relationship with the person who has a substance use problem, or in other relationships.

Some people find it confusing when they try on one hand to support and love the person who uses substances, and on the other hand to simultaneously set limits. Ask the group members if and how setting limits can be consistent with loving and supporting behaviour. How can setting limits help the person who has a substance use problem?

PRACTISING DETERMINING BOUNDARIES AND LIMITS

Do one or both of the two following exercises. If you choose not to do Exercise 2 during the session, encourage the group members to try it at home.

Exercise 1

▶ **Draw an imaginary line within the room. Place a sign at one end that reads, "I will tolerate . . ." and a sign at the other end that reads, "I will not tolerate. . . ." Tell the participants that you will read descriptions of various situations or behaviours, and ask them to place themselves somewhere on the line to indicate what they will and will not tolerate.**

Emphasize that everyone has different boundaries and sets different limits, and that there is no right and wrong. Encourage the group members to make their own decisions, but to notice where they are in relation to others. Read some of the situations listed below, or create your own.

· My neighbour asks to borrow my car to drive her child to the hospital.
· My friend comes over for dinner uninvited because she has no money for food, due to drinking.
· My brother asks to borrow the car in order to drive to his substance use treatment sessions.
· My friend drops off her children for babysitting when she has been drinking.
· My partner, who is high, calls me from work to tell me that he will not be coming home tonight.
· My partner, who is high, calls me from work to ask for a ride.
· My partner calls me from a bar at 2:30 a.m. He is drunk.
· My father calls me when he is hung over and asks that I come over and make him lunch.
· My son smokes pot on the porch of our house.
· My son smokes pot in his room in our house.
· My son smokes pot in the living room of our house.
· My partner gets drunk when we celebrate our anniversary.
· My daughter takes money out of my wallet.
· My partner leaves drug paraphernalia in the bathroom.
· My son demands that I make him some supper at 1:00 a.m.

· My son punches a hole in the wall during an angry outburst.
· My daughter swears at me when I ask her to clean up after herself.
· My partner asks me to drive him to medical and therapy appointments to ensure that he goes.
· My partner pays little attention to the children when in withdrawal.
· My daughter asks me to drive her to the hospital to get a prescription, which I believe she will abuse.
· My sister asks me to look for substance use treatment programs for her.
· Drug dealers come to the house asking for my son.
· My son asks me to pay off his debt at a local bar so that he is not beaten up.
· My daughter calls to inform me that she has been using drugs and asks that I look after her children.
· My partner throws objects because he is angry with me for interfering with his substance use.
· My mother calls me from a treatment facility begging me to take her home.
· My partner, who is not working, does not help out around the home.
· My sister calls me periodically, telling me that she has cut herself.
· My father lives with us because he has lost his job and has been evicted from his apartment for not paying rent.

Following this exercise, you may wish to discuss what factors might influence whether people tolerate or do not tolerate the behaviour (e.g., one's relationship to or history with the person, the frequency or chronicity of the behaviour, fears for the safety of the person).

Discuss the importance of being flexible regarding boundaries, yet consistent and firm when setting limits with individuals. Flexibility is needed because family members' comfort levels, needs and behaviour might change in different situations (e.g., at work versus at home), at different times (e.g., on the weekend, during the night, during vacations), with different demands (e.g., a request to borrow a car, a spontaneous visit) and with different people (a partner, a child who does not use substances, a child who uses substances). As a result, a person's boundaries may vary.

It is nonetheless crucial to be consistent and firm when one has set a specific limit with a specific person in a specific situation, and outlined the consequences of breaking that limit. For example, a person might be willing in general to have her children drop in spontaneously for meals, but may decide that she will ask one of her children to leave if she has already come for a meal three times that week, or if she has been drinking.

Exercise 2

▶ **Distribute or turn to Handout 15-2: Determining My Boundaries and ask the group members to spend five minutes completing it.**

Emphasize that everyone has different boundaries and limits and that there is no right or wrong. The examples in the handout may not reflect their own limits. Explain that this exercise is about determining what one will tolerate, which is the first step in setting and enforcing limits.

BARRIERS TO PROTECTING BOUNDARIES AND SETTING LIMITS

Discuss what often gets in the way of setting limits. If helpful, refer to Handout 15-3: Barriers to Protecting Common Boundaries.

SETTING LIMITS

Ask the participants for tips about how to communicate in a way that will increase the likelihood of the person with a substance use problem hearing their message.

▶ **Distribute or turn to Handout 15-4: Communicating Loving Limits, and Handout 15-5: Communicating Limits Using the DESC Model.**

These tips are similar to those discussed in Module 10: Communicating Effectively with a Person Who Has a Substance Use Problem. If you have not presented this module, spend time discussing each tip. If you have covered Module 10, give the handout as a reference and review the tips briefly.

▶ **Distribute or turn to Handout 15-6: Setting Loving Limits. Ask the group members to spend five minutes working on this handout.**

Suggest that they look at their list of what they will not tolerate, from Handout 15-2, and choose a limit that would be mildly difficult to enforce (i.e, not something at the top of their list).

Ask the group members to share their plans with each other.

Explain that it is important that they stick to their plan and that they be consistent in their responses and in administering consequences (if necessary). They will be more likely to succeed if they act with consistency and do not give in, even once in a while. Group members should be prepared for the person with a substance use problem to test the limit and possibly to behave worse. If they stick to their plan and continue to enforce the limit when things are worse, they will eventually succeed in convincing the person that they are serious. Discuss the importance of choosing a consequence that they can follow through on.

Acknowledge the reality that setting limits is difficult and may be risky. Group members will have to figure out for themselves what risks they are willing to tolerate. Advise them always to be cautious about setting a limit with a person who has a substance use problem if they anticipate that the person could become violent.

Home practice

Direct the group members to try communicating a limit to the person who has a substance use problem, and enforcing that limit.

Boundaries and limits

WHY HAVE BOUNDARIES?

Boundaries exist to PROTECT yourself and others:

Prevent resentment and/or burnout.

Reduce abuse, exploitation, dominance or control by another.

Overcome unhelpful and unsustainable patterns of relating.

Take responsibility only for what is your responsibility.

Express needs.

Care for yourself physically, sexually and emotionally.

Try to model healthy boundaries.

HOW DO YOU PROTECT YOUR BOUNDARIES?

STOP to determine, set and enforce limits:

Set limits on another person's behaviour with respect to your boundaries.

Tell the person of these limits and the consequences if the limits are not respected.

Observe whether the person is respecting these limits.

Proceed by following through on the consequences if your limits have not been respected.

Determining my boundaries

BEHAVIOUR OF A PERSON WITH A SUBSTANCE USE PROBLEM

Fill in some situations in each of the columns to help determine what you will and will not tolerate. Everyone has different limits and is in a different situation, so use the examples only as a guide, not as a prescription about what you should or should not tolerate.

I WILL TOLERATE . . .	I AM UNSURE IF I WILL TOLERATE . . .	I WILL NOT TOLERATE . . .
Example: My partner calling me when high, if it is to tell me that he will not be coming home tonight Example: My sister using my car to get to substance use treatment	Example: My father drinking at holiday dinners Example: My daughter calling me for a ride when intoxicated	Example: My partner using drugs in the house Example: My son losing his temper and damaging my home

Common barriers to protecting boundaries

LACK OF SKILLS
· not knowing how to set a limit
· communicating ineffectively with another person about a limit

LACK OF AWARENESS
· not being aware of your own feelings, needs and boundaries
· not noticing when your boundaries are being violated

FEELINGS
· fear about how the person will respond
· guilt for not being more tolerant of the person
· hurt that the person does not automatically know and respect your boundaries
· discomfort with expressing or asserting your needs
· fear about the costs and risks of setting limits

EXPECTATIONS AND BELIEFS
· belief that you do not have the right to demand that your boundaries
  be respected
· belief that setting limits is selfish and not loving
· expectation that the other person should already know and respect
  your limits
· expectation that you will not follow through on the consequences you have
  set, if your limits are not respected

   Therefore to protect your boundaries and remain SAFE, you must examine
whether you need to develop Skills, increase your Awareness, modify your
Feelings or change your Expectations.

Communicating loving limits

CHOOSE AN APPROPRIATE TIME
· Choose a time when the person with a substance use problem is not drinking alcohol, using other substances or hung over.
· Choose a time when you and the other person are both calm.
· Choose a time when you and the other person are not in a hurry.

CHOOSE A NEUTRAL PLACE
· Choose a place that is not associated with substance use or with fights.
· Choose a place where you will be safe.

DEMONSTRATE UNDERSTANDING
Verbalize the feelings, thoughts and behaviours of the person that make sense to you.

TAKE RESPONSIBILITY
· Use "I" statements when talking about your feelings.
· Take responsibility for any way in which you contribute to the problem.
· Offer to contribute to solving the problem or to change your behaviour.

BE POSITIVE
· Word your requests in a positive way.
· Avoid sweeping negative statements about the person who has a substance use problem.
· Avoid general statements such as "you never" or "you always."

BE FIRM
· Do not apologize for or defend your limits.
· Be a "broken record" if necessary.
· Stay focused on your goal (do not let your emotions or an argument derail you).

BE SPECIFIC
· Specify your limits.
· Specify what you would like the other person to do.
· Specify what the consequences will be if he or she does not respect your limits.

Communicating limits using the DESC model

Use the DESC model to help you speak specifically, positively and assertively.

Describe the situation: "When you . . ." (behaviour)

Express your feelings: "I feel . . ." (emotion)

Specify what you want: "I would like / prefer . . ." (need/desire)

Communicate the consequences: "I will . . ." (positive payoff)
           "You will . . ." (positive payoff)
           "If . . . then . . ." (consequences
           should the limit not be respected).

Adapted from Bower, S. & Bower, A. (2004). *Asserting Yourself: A Practical Guide for Positive Change.* Cambridge, MA: Da Capo Press.

EXAMPLES

When you drink after you have come home, I feel hurt and lonely, and miss the times we share when you are sober. I'd like to hang out with you in the evenings and I know that our relationship will improve if we do. I've decided that if you start drinking when you come home from work, I'll go out and spend time with a friend.

When you use drugs, I worry a lot about you. I love who you are and I fear what the drugs are doing to you. I'd like you to be able to continue living here while you're going to university, but I've decided that I'll only allow you to stay here as long as I see no signs of you using drugs. From now on, if I find drugs or drug paraphernalia in the apartment, or if I see you using drugs or being high, I'll give you one month to find a new place to live.

I've noticed that when you call our kids when you're drunk, they can tell and they become angry and worried about you. I'd like you to call us only when you're sober. I think that we'll all have a better relationship with you if we talk to you when you're sober. I've decided that for their sake, I'll answer all the phone calls and won't pass them the phone if I can tell that you've been drinking.

Setting loving limits

Choose a behaviour that you are not willing to tolerate, and decide how you
will communicate and enforce this limit:

_____

Limit I would like to set:

_____

_____

Where I will communicate this limit:

_____

When I will communicate this limit:

_____

How I will communicate this limit (what I will say): use the DESC model
as a guide.

D = _____

E = _____

S = _____

C = _____

Possible responses of my relative to this limit:

_____

_____

Consequences if my relative does not respect this limit:

_____

_____

How I did in setting the limit and sticking with it this week:

_____

_____

Helping children affected by substance use in the family

OBJECTIVES

· to provide a supportive environment in which group members can discuss their concerns about the children and adolescents in their lives
· to help group members identify the effects of familial substance use on children and adolescents
· to present and discuss ways to reduce the effects of familial substance use on children and adolescents
· to help group members increase the resilience of children and adolescents affected by substance use

HANDOUTS

16-1: How to Help Children Affected by Substance Use Problems
16-2: Supporting Children Affected by Substance Use Problems
16-3: Books for Parents, Children and Adolescents

SESSION OUTLINE

· Opening and announcements (approx. 5 min.)
· Check-in and review of last week's home practice (approx. 30 min.)
· Teaching and discussion (approx. 60 min.)
· Assigning of next week's home practice (approx. 5 min.)
· Closing (approx. 5 min.)

Teaching and discussion

We recommend that you remind group members prior to this session of the limits of confidentiality (See Module 1: Starting Out). In particular, restate your need to report to child welfare authorities if you find out that a child is being harmed or is at risk of harm.

EFFECTS OF FAMILIAL SUBSTANCE USE ON CHILDREN

Ask the group members how many children they have, and their ages (or, if they have no children, how many younger siblings, nieces or nephews, or other younger relatives they have who may have been affected by familial substance use). Ask how the presence of substance use problems in the family has affected these children and adolescents. Ask them to share their fears with regard to the effects of the substance use on these children.

▶ **You may choose to write down the responses on a blackboard, whiteboard or flipchart.**

Here are some examples of difficulties of children whose parents use substances, found within the research literature (sources are provided in the References section of this module):

· increased risk of abuse or neglect
· increased risk of family disruption, unstable housing and poverty
· "parentification" of children (i.e., taking on adult responsibilities, such as rescuing or protecting a parent) or early independence from parents, before the children are developmentally prepared for such roles
· isolation due both to protecting the family secret regarding the substance use and to shame about the substance use
· burying or acting out feelings related to the substance use, because they are not allowed to express their feelings
· embarrassment due to the behaviour of the person with a substance use problem
· perceived or actual stigma because of their relative's substance use
· confusion due to their relative's inconsistent behaviour, messages and limit setting
· increased incidence of anxiety, depression, behaviour problems and delinquency

· early exposure to, knowledge of and involvement with criminal and illegal activity
· increased incidence of alcohol and other drug use themselves.

Although research has shown higher rates of the above problems for children affected by familial substance use, it is important to assure the group members that such effects are not guaranteed. Explain that families affected by substance use problems are highly disparate, and differ with regard to strengths (e.g., consistent caring and an involved parent, social support) and other problems (e.g., poverty, instability, violence, mental health problems), so the family experience will vary considerably. Similarly, children—even those whose situations are similar—are all different and deal with familial substance use (and other problems) in varying ways. Some children are more resilient than others because of their temperament, intelligence, family relationships and other factors.

We advise that you be realistic with the group members about the difficulties faced by these children and that you encourage them to look below the surface of children who are apparently doing well, to explore whether they are struggling internally and perhaps denying or hiding their problems and feelings. Nonetheless, do not be unnecessarily pessimistic or dwell on this topic for too long. We recommend that you focus on how to help these children, which is within their caregivers' control and can motivate them to helpful action.

HELPING CHILDREN

Ask the group members what they have tried to do to help their children deal with the situation.

▶ **Distribute or turn to Handout 16-1: How to Help Children Affected by Substance Use Problems.**

Explain that research has identified factors that help children do well despite difficult childhood circumstances (such as substance use problems in the family) and factors that prevent children themselves from developing substance use problems. The list of recommendations in Handout 16-1 is based on current research on these protective and preventative factors. A list of relevant articles and books is included in the "References" section (see page 301).

Read through the suggestions together and discuss them as a group. Ask the group members if they or other caregivers are already doing some of these things. If there are certain recommendations that are particularly salient, problematic, controversial or difficult for the group members to follow, spend time discussing them at greater length. Respond to the needs of the group as you go through this section. For example, you may want to spend time discussing the pros and cons of a particular suggestion, the experiences of others in - implementing a suggestion, the rationale for a suggestion or barriers to implementing suggestions.

ENSURING CHILDREN'S SAFETY

Stress the importance of children's safety and the group members' (or any adult's) responsibility to ensure that children are safe. Emphasize that children are much less likely to be resilient in dealing with familial substance use if they have been abused or neglected. Brainstorm with the group on ways to keep children safe.

If you are concerned about the safety of a child, ask to speak with the group member following the group. Information that might alert you to possible safety issues includes the following:

· Children may be witnessing domestic violence.

· Children may be observing caregivers using substances.

· Children are being left in the care of a caregiver (e.g., at home or during a visit) who may be using a substance. This may be a problem even if the person waits until the children are sleeping to use substances, or does so out of the home and then returns high or inebriated.

· Children are being driven by a caregiver who may be under the influence of a substance.

· Children may be the recipients of verbal or physical abuse because of how a caregiver might behave in general or when using or withdrawing from a substance.

· Children might not be cared for adequately because of a caregiver's preoccupation with obtaining and using substances (e.g., they may have inadequate food, supervision, shelter or medical services).

· Children might be sexually abused or exposed to sexually inappropriate material.

· Children might be involved in some way in a caregiver's use or acquisition of substances (e.g., picking up drugs, paying a dealer, delivering drugs, helping prepare substances).

· Children might be assuming developmentally inappropriate roles and responsibilities within the family (e.g., caring emotionally for a parent, cleaning up after a parent, looking after younger siblings).

· Children might be exhibiting clinically significant emotional, behavioural, academic or social problems.

TALKING ABOUT SUBSTANCE USE

Ask the group members if they have spoken with the children in their family about the familial substance use. If they have, ask:

· Why did you speak to them about the familial substance use?

· How did you speak to them?

· How did the conversation go?

· How much had the children or adolescents known and believed about the familial substance use, prior to your conversation?

If the group members have not openly talked to the children about the familial substance use, ask:

· Why have you not spoken to them?

· What do you think they already know and believe about the familial substance use, or about the person who has a substance use problem?

· Do you plan to speak to them about the substance use in the future and, if so, when (i.e., what are you waiting for)?

· What concerns do you have about speaking to them?

If there is debate among group members about talking to children about the substance use, discuss people's opinions and consider the pros and cons of talking and not talking about it. Often it is fear, shame or discomfort that prevents caregivers from talking to children about this issue. Emphasize that children often know more than we think about familial substance use and, unless we speak about it openly, they may misunderstand the behaviour, blame themselves, feel shame, or not know how to express feelings and voice concerns about it.

MANAGING DIFFICULT EMOTIONS AND SITUATIONS

We recommend that you also emphasize the importance of helping children deal with difficult emotions. Many adults struggle with this themselves, and so do not know how to teach their children these skills. Although people differ with regard to their emotional sensitivity, we all can learn ways of calming ourselves, managing our emotions and problem solving. If you have presented any of Module 9: Managing Emotions, you can refer back to some of the ideas discussed there. Together you can think of emotion management methods that could be helpful to the children in the group members' lives. Some approaches suitable for children include:

· expressing difficult feelings and thoughts through talking, writing, drawing or making music

- distracting themselves from the feelings if they are too overwhelming, by engaging in an entertaining or fun activity (e.g., watching a movie, playing sports, pursuing a craft, dancing)
- calming themselves by deep breathing, visualization, counting, taking a time out, having a bath, listening to relaxing music or having a hug
- finding an adult they trust and with whom they can seek comfort, express feelings, voice concerns and ask questions.

If parents have difficulties in these areas, encourage them to get help themselves by reading books, attending workshops or seeing a therapist, so they can model and teach the children in their lives appropriate means of managing difficult emotions. They can also help their children by giving them relevant books, showing them relevant websites and seeking professional resources when necessary.

In addition to helping children manage difficult emotions, group members need to help children deal with difficult situations, in part through effective problem solving. If you have completed Module 11: Problem Solving, you can refer back to that session. If not, you could briefly teach them the problem-solving method outlined there so they can in turn teach it to the children in their lives. Emphasize that even preschool children can learn how to problem solve with assistance, and that being a good problem solver can help a child become more resilient.

▶ **Distribute or turn to Handout 16-2: Supporting Children Affected by Substance Use Problems.**

Ask the group members to use the handout to help identify something supportive that they are already doing for the children in their families, and something else that they would like to work on. Spend time helping them develop a plan to implement this suggestion, being sure to consider what barriers there might be and how to overcome them.

ACCESSING RESOURCES

Discuss how to recognize when a child needs mental health services. Considerations include:
- the severity of symptoms
- the duration of symptoms
- the effect of symptoms on the child's functioning (e.g., school failure, lack of friends, legal problems)
- the difficulties for the parent in managing the child's symptoms

· requests for help by the child
· recommendations by others (e.g., a teacher) that the child receive help.

Give the group members a list of resources for child and adolescent prevention and mental health services in your area. Give them time to ask questions about the process of seeking services for children.

Encourage the participants to improve their ability to care for children by reading books, attending parenting classes or workshops, and talking with friends and family members about their children and their parenting.

▶ **Distribute or turn to Handout 16-3: Books for Parents, Children and Adolescents.**

Home practice

Ask the group members to implement one of the suggestions for helping children affected by familial substance use.

References

Beardslee, W.R., Versage, E.M. & Gladstone, T.R.G. (1998). Children of affectively ill parents: A review of the past 10 years. *Journal of the American Academy of Child and Adolescent Psychiatry, 37* (11), 1134–1141.

Biederman, J., Faraone, S.V. & Monuteauz, M.C. (2002). Impact of exposure to parental attention-deficit hyperactivity disorder on clinical features and dysfunction in the offspring. *Psychological Medicine, 32* (5), 817–827.

Black, C. (2003). *Straight Talk from Claudia Black: What Recovering Parents Should Tell Their Kids about Drugs and Alcohol.* Center City, MN: Hazelden.

Centre for Addiction and Mental Health. (2006). *Strengthening Families for the Future.* Toronto: Author.

Chassin, L., Pitts, S.C., DeLucia, C. & Todd, M. (1999). A longitudinal study of children of alcoholics: Predicting young adult substance use disorders, anxiety, and depression. *Journal of Abnormal Psychology, 108* (1), 106–119.

Christensen, H.B. & Bilenberg, N. (2000). Behavioural and emotional problems in children of alcoholic mothers and fathers. *European Child and Adolescent Psychiatry, 9,* 219–226.

Harbin, F. & Murphy, M. (2000). Substance misuse and child care: How to understand, assist and intervene when drugs affect parenting. Lyme Regis, U.K.: Russell House Publishing.

Kelley, M.L. & Fals-Stewart, W. (2004), Psychiatric disorders of children living with drug-abusing, alcohol-abusing and non-substance-abusing fathers. *Journal of the American Academy of Child and Adolescent Psychiatry, 43* (5), 621–628.

Leverton, T.J. (2003). Parental psychiatric illness: The implications for children. *Current Opinion in Psychiatry, 16* (4), 395–402.

Nastasi, B.K. & DeZolt, D.M. (1994). *School Interventions for Children of Alcoholics*. New York: Guilford Press.

Nomura, Y., Warner, V. & Wickramaratne, P. (2001). Parents concordant for major depressive disorder and the effect of psychopathology in offspring. *Psychological Medicine, 31* (7), 1211–1222.

Robinson, B.E. & Rhoden, J.L. (1998). *Working with Children of Alcoholics: The Practitioner's Handbook* (2nd ed.). Thousand Oaks, CA: Sage Publications.

Schwebel, R. (1998). *Saying No Is Not Enough: Helping Your Kids Make Wise Decisions about Alcohol, Tobacco, and Other Drugs—A Guide for Parents of Children Ages 3 through 19* (2nd ed.). New York: Newmarket Press.

Scottish Executive. (2003). *Getting Our Priorities Right: Good Practice Guidance for Working with Children and Families Affected by Substance Misuse.* Available: www.scotland.gov.uk/Publications/2003/02/16469/18705. Accessed December 17, 2007.

How to help children affected by substance use problems

OBTAIN TREATMENT OR SUPPORT FOR YOURSELF
· Learn about alcohol and other drugs, and their effects on the family.
· Learn ways of coping with difficult emotions and with the person who has a substance use problem.
· Learn good parenting strategies.
· Talk to people outside of the family for support.

ENSURE CHILDREN'S SAFETY
· Do not permit family members to misuse alcohol or to use other drugs in the presence of the children or when supervising them.
· If concerned about safety, arrange for the children's visits with the family member who has a substance use problem to be supervised.
· Help the children develop a safety plan.
· Ensure that the children do not take on a parental role in the family.
· Watch for signs of abuse or neglect.
· Call child welfare authorities (e.g., the Children's Aid Society) if a child is being harmed or at risk of harm.

COMMUNICATE WITH CHILDREN ABOUT SUBSTANCE USE
· Talk with the children about alcohol and other drugs.
· Talk with them about their relative's substance use.
· Tell them that they are not to blame for the person's subtance use and are not responsible for fixing the problem.

HELP CHILDREN DEAL WITH DIFFICULT EMOTIONS AND SITUATIONS
· Model effective ways of expressing and managing your emotions and of calming yourself.
· Help the children learn effective ways to express and manage their own feelings and to calm themselves.
· Model effective ways to solve problems.
· Help the children to learn effective ways to solve problems.
· Get mental health treatment for the children, if necessary.
· Encourage them to talk to others about their difficulties.

BE INVOLVED AND CONSISTENT

· Ensure adequate supervision of the children.
· Set reasonable expectations and limits for them, and follow through on consequences you have set.
· Allow them to experience the consequences of their behaviour (including the consequences of experimenting with or using substances).
· Spend time together (e.g., eating meals, going for walks, reading).

PROVIDE RESPONSIVE AND POSITIVE CARE

· Listen to and validate the children.
· Respond to their feelings and needs.
· Provide them with positive feedback and encouragement.
· Tell them and show them that they are loved.

HELP CHILDREN TO DEVELOP POSITIVE RELATIONSHIPS WITH OTHERS

· Foster good relationships between the children and other family members (including, if possible, the person with a substance use problem).
· Have fun together as a family.
· Encourage the children to take part in cultural, religious or community-based events.
· Provide many opportunities for them to develop friendships and learn social skills.
· Encourage them to socialize with peers who do not use alcohol or other drugs.

ENCOURAGE AND FOSTER CHILDREN'S SUCCESS

· Allow the children to make decisions about their lives.
· Encourage them to be involved in meaningful activities and hobbies.
· Reinforce their academic achievements.
· Encourage them to contribute to the family and community.
· Help them to develop a cultural and community-based identity.
· Support their goals and aspirations.
· Believe in them.

Supporting children affected by substance use problems

Identify what you are doing that is supportive and helpful:

_____

_____

_____

Identify one suggestion that you would like to put into action this week:

_____

Plan what you will do to put this suggestion into action:

_____

_____

_____

Plan when you will put the suggestion into action:

_____

Consider anything that will prevent you from putting this plan into action. How will you overcome these barriers?

_____

_____

_____

Record how you did:

_____

_____

Record the child's or adolescent's response:

_____

Books for parents, children and adolescents

PARENTING CHILDREN AFFECTED BY A PARENT'S SUBSTANCE USE

Black, C. (2003). *Straight Talk from Claudia Black: What Recovering Parents Should Tell Their Kids about Drugs and Alcohol.* Center City, MN: Hazelden.

Wood, B. (2002). *Raising Healthy Children in an Alcoholic Home* (2nd ed.). Center City, MN: Hazelden.

PREVENTING SUBSTANCE USE BY CHILDREN

Kuhn, C., Swarzwelder, S. & Wilson, W. (2002). *Just Say Know: Talking with Kids about Drugs and Alcohol.* New York: W.W. Norton.

Schwebel, R. (1998). *Saying No Is Not Enough: Helping Your Kids Make Wise Decisions about Alcohol, Tobacco, and Other Drugs—A Guide for Parents of Children Ages 3 through 19* (2nd ed.). New York: Newmarket Press.

Wilmes, D. (1995). *Parenting for Prevention: How to Raise a Child to say No to Alcohol/Drugs* (rev. ed.). Center City, MN: Hazelden.

PARENTING CHILDREN WHEN STRUGGLING WITH MENTAL HEALTH PROBLEMS

McKay, M., Fanning, P., Paleg, K. & Landis, D. (1997). *When Anger Hurts Your Kids: A Parent's Guide.* Oakland, CA: New Harbinger Publications.

Nicholson, J., Henry, A., Clayfield, J. & Phillips, S. (2001). *Parenting Well When You're Depressed: A Complete Resource for Maintaining a Healthy Family.* Oakland, CA: New Harbinger Publications.

Yapko, M. (1999). *Hand Me Down Blues: How to Stop Depression from Spreading in Families.* New York: St. Martin's Press.

PARENTING CHILDREN AFFECTED BY SEPARATION

McDonough, H. & Bartha, C. (1999). *Putting Children First: A Guide for Parents Breaking Up.* Toronto: University of Toronto Press.

PARENTING CHILDREN EXHIBITING EMOTIONAL OR
BEHAVIOURAL DIFFICULTIES

Barkley, R. & Benton, C. (1998). *Your Defiant Child*. New York: Guilford Press.

Carducci, B. & Kaiser, L. (2003). *The Shyness Breakthrough*. New York: St. Martin's Press.

Chamsky, T. (2004). *Freeing Your Child from Anxiety*. New York: Broadway Books.

Forehand, R. & Long, N. (2002). *Parenting the Strong-Willed Child: The Clinically Proven Five-Week Program for Parents of Two- to Six-Year-Olds* (rev. ed.). New York: McGraw Hill.

Manassis, K. (1996). *Keys to Parenting Your Anxious Child*. New York: Barron's Educational Series.

Sells, S. (2002). *Parenting Your Out of Control Teenager*. New York: St. Martin's Press.

SUBSTANCE USE AND MENTAL HEALTH ISSUES FOR CHILDREN

Black, C. (1997). *My Dad Loves Me, My Dad Has a Disease* (3rd ed.). San Francisco, CA: Mac Publishing.

Centre for Addiction and Mental Health. (2002). *Can I Catch It Like a Cold? A Story to Help Children Understand a Parent's Depression*. Toronto: Author.

Centre for Addiction and Mental Health. (2005). *Wishes and Worries: A Story to Help Children Understand a Parent Who Drinks Too Much*. Toronto: Author.

Hamilton, D. & Owens, G. (1995). *Sad Days, Glad Days: A Story about Depression*. Morton Grove, IL: Albert Whitman and Company.

Hastings, J. (1994). *An Elephant in the Living Room: The Children's Book*. Center City, MN: Hazelden.

Helmer, D.S. (1999). *Let's Talk about When Your Mom or Dad Is Unhappy*. Center City, MN: Hazelden.

Johnston, M. (1998). *Let's Talk about Alcohol Abuse*. Center City, MN: Hazelden.

Kreiner, A. (1998). *Let's Talk about Drug Abuse*. Center City, MN: Hazelden.

Mercury, C. (1997). *Think of Wind*. Rochester, NY: One Big Press.

Moore Campbell, B. (2003). *Sometimes My Mommy Gets Angry*. New York: G.P. Putnam's Sons.

Vigna, J. (1993). *I Wish Daddy Didn't Drink So Much*. Morton Grove, IL: Albert Whitman and Company.

Vigna, J. (1995). *My Big Sister Takes Drugs*. Morton Grove, IL: Albert Whitman and Company.

SUBSTANCE USE AND MENTAL HEALTH ISSUES FOR ADOLESCENTS

Black, C. (2001). *It Will Never Happen to Me: Growing Up with Addiction as Youngsters, Adolescents, Adults*. Center City, MN: Hazelden.

Brennfleck Shannon, J. (2005). *Alcohol Information for Teens: Health Tips about Alcohol and Alcoholism*. Detroit, MI: Omnigraphics.

Crist, J. (2003). *When Someone You Love Abuses Alcohol or Drugs: A Guide for Kids*. Winnipeg, MB: Wellness Institute.

Hipp, E. (1995). *Help for the Hard Times: Getting through Loss*. Center City, MN: Hazelden.

Hornik-Beer, E. (2001). *For Teenagers Living with a Parent Who Abuses Alcohol/Drugs*. New York: Backinprint.com.

McFarland, R. (1997). *Drugs and Your Brothers and Sisters* (rev. ed.). Rosen Publishing Group.

Miller, S. (1995). *When Parents Have Problems: A Book for Teens and Older Children with an Abusive, Alcoholic, or Mentally Ill Parent*. Springfield, IL: C.C. Thomas.

O'Toole, D. (1995). *Facing Change: Falling Apart and Coming Together Again in the Teen Years*. Burnsville, NC: Compassion Press.

Rosenberg, E. (2002). *Growing Up Feeling Good: The Life Handbook for Kids* (rev. ed.). Long Beach, NY: Lima Bean Press.

PARENTING IN GENERAL

Borba, M. (1999). *Parents Do Make a Difference: How to Raise Kids with Solid Character, Strong Minds and Caring Hearts*. San Francisco, CA: Jossey-Bass.

Christopherson, E. & Mortweet, S. (2003). *Parenting That Works*. Washington, DC: APA Life Tools.

Clark, L. (1996). *SOS! Help for Parents*, Bowling Green, KY: Parents Press.

Coloroso, B. (2002). *Kids Are Worth It! Giving Your Child the Gift of Inner Discipline*. New York: HarperCollins.

Faber, A. & Mazlish, E. (1999). *How to Talk So Kids Will Listen and Listen So Kids Will Talk* (2nd ed.). New York: Avon Books.

Pantley, E. (1996). *Kid Cooperation: How to Stop Yelling, Nagging and Pleading and Get Kids to Cooperate*. Oakland, CA: New Harbinger.

Severe, S. (2001). *How to Behave So Your Preschooler Will Too*. New York: Penguin.

Severe, S. (2003). *How to Behave So Your Children Will Too*. New York: Penguin.

Webster–Stratton, C. (2002). *The Incredible Years: A Trouble-Shooting Guide for Parents of Children Aged 3–8*. Toronto: Umbrella Press.

WEBSITES FOR CHILDREN, YOUTH AND PARENTS

Al-Anon/Alateen: www.al-anon.alateen.org

Children of Alcoholics Foundation (COAF): www.coaf.org

Family Association for Mental Health Everywhere (FAME): www.fameforfamilies.com

Freevibe.com: www.freevibe.com

National Association for Children of Alcoholics (NACOA): www.nacoa.org

National Institute of Drug Abuse: www.teens.drugabuse.gov/

Puberty 101: www.puberty101.com

Finding hope

OBJECTIVES

· to help group members be mindful of their past and current hopefulness
· to provide information about ways of increasing hopefulness
· to help group members realize that they can feel hopeful about their situation and themselves even when not hopeful about their relative's recovery
· to encourage group members to increase their hopefulness

HANDOUTS

17-1: Finding Hope Survey
17-2: How to Modify Hopefulness
17-3: Increasing Hope
17-4: Sayings Related to Hopefulness

SESSION OUTLINE

· Opening and announcements (approx. 5 min.)
· Check-in and review of last week's home practice (approx. 30 min.)
· Teaching and discussion (approx. 60 min.)
· Assigning of next week's home practice (approx. 5 min.)
· Closing (approx. 5 min.)

Teaching and discussion

DEFINING HOPEFULNESS

Ask the group members to define hopefulness. Discuss what hope is:

> To cherish a desire with anticipation; to desire with expectation of obtainment; to expect with confidence (Merriam-Webster Dictionary).

Discuss what hope is not:
· false cheerfulness
· naive optimism
· a way to mask discouragement
· a way to deny reality (or to collude in denying reality with the person who has a substance use problem).

Ask the group members to discuss what it is like to have hope.

▶ **Distribute or turn to Handout 17-1: Finding Hope Survey. Ask the group members to complete the first four questions of this survey.**

HOW DO WE EXPERIENCE HOPE?

Hopefulness can manifest in various ways:
· emotionally: feeling excited, encouraged, confident
· cognitively: predicting positive outcomes, thinking optimistically, making future plans, acknowledging your own abilities
· spiritually: believing in a higher power, believing that God cares, believing in the goodness of humanity, believing that someone cares, believing that help is available
· behaviourally: taking steps, making changes, persisting, patting yourself on the back
· interpersonally: involving others, being aware of the help you are receiving, maintaining or fostering relationships.

HOW DOES IT FEEL TO LOSE HOPE?

Ask the group members to discuss what it is like not to have hope.

Hopelessness can manifest in various ways:

· emotionally: feeling depressed, discouraged, stressed
· cognitively: predicting negative outcomes, thinking pessimistically, giving up, wanting to die
· spiritually: not believing in God or a higher power, not believing that God cares, not believing in the goodness of humanity, not believing that help is available
· behaviourally: becoming passive, trying nothing, sabotaging progress
· interpersonally: withdrawing, being critical, giving up on relationships.

HOPE AND RECOVERY

Explain that the ability to develop or maintain a hopeful attitude helps to predict who will recover or who will benefit from treatment, and who will survive difficult experiences.

Emphasize the importance of hope for group members as they participate in this group and in their own journey toward recovery.

▶ **Turn again to Handout 17-1: Finding Hope Survey.**

Ask the group members to share what they feel hopeful about.

▶ **Discuss what circumstances increase hope and what ones decrease hope. Write the group's answers on a blackboard, whiteboard or flipchart.**

Discuss what factors group members have within their control. Explain that what happens to the person who has a substance use problem will inevitably affect them. Nonetheless they need to be able to maintain hope even if their relative's situation deteriorates. There are events in one's life (e.g., job loss, separation, the death of a loved one) that often contribute to increased feelings of hopelessness. However, this feeling is often temporary. Its level varies from person to person, based on how the individual copes with adversity.

▶ **Distribute or turn to Handout 17-2: How to Modify Hopefulness.**

Go over any points that have not come up in the previous discussions. These factors are within participants' control and can help them to maintain or increase hope, even within a difficult situation.

▶ **Distribute or turn to Handout 17-3: Increasing Hope. Ask the participants to answer the questions on Handout 17-3, using Handout 17-2 as a guide.**

Then ask them to return to Handout 17-1 and to complete the final questions.

Discuss with the group members what they intend to do to work on increasing their hopefulness in the upcoming week.

Recovery success stories

If you have time, you may wish to invite a former group member to the group to share his or her story of success. The person's story need not necessarily relate to how his or her relative did; rather, it could relate to how the former participant coped, survived and remained hopeful through the experience.

Alternatively, you could ask the participants to share their own stories of success.

▶ **Distribute or turn to Handout 17-4: Sayings Related to Hopefulness.**

Ask the group members if they have a favourite saying or quotation that instils hopefulness in them. If not, ask them to create or find one, or choose one from the list, to recite daily to themselves during the week. You may suggest that they write the quotation in a place where they will regularly see it. Ask the group members to read aloud the quotations on Handout 17-4.

Home practice

Ask the participants to try to increase their hopefulness during the week by focusing on changing one aspect of their thinking or behaviour.

Finding hope survey

1. How hopeful did you feel when you started this group?

1	2	3	4	5
Not at all hopeful	Somewhat hopeful	Moderately hopeful	Quite hopeful	Very hopeful

2. What did you feel hopeful about?

_____

_____

_____

3. How hopeful do you feel now?

1	2	3	4	5
Not at all hopeful	Somewhat hopeful	Moderately hopeful	Quite hopeful	Very hopeful

4. What do you feel hopeful about?

_____

_____

_____

5. What may have contributed to the increase, decrease or lack of change in your degree of hopefulness from the time you began the group until now?

_____

_____

_____

6. What do you think you could do to maintain your level of hopefulness or to become more hopeful?

_____

_____

_____

How to modify hopefulness

WHAT CAN INCREASE HOPEFULNESS

		EXAMPLE
Thoughts	Optimism	"I believe that my situation will improve."
		"I believe that treatment will be helpful."
	Self-mastery and self-efficacy	"I believe that I can improve my situation."
	Self-encouragement	"I can do it. I can make these changes. I am a good person."
	Creativity	"I can think of many ways to deal with any problem or get around any obstacle."
Behaviour	Achieving goals	Attaining success in making small steps toward my goals
	Reinforcing myself	Patting myself on the back
		Feeling good about myself
	Positive experiences	Enjoying time with others
		Engaging in activities that are pleasurable
	Learning from others	Hearing how others have survived or overcome difficult circumstances

WHAT CAN DECREASE HOPEFULNESS
(INCREASE HOPELESSNESS)

		EXAMPLE
THOUGHTS	All or nothing thinking	"I made one slip, therefore I have completely failed."
	Catastrophic thinking	"The worst will happen and I will not be able to cope."
	Negative self-talk	"I can't do anything right."
	Helplessness	"There is nothing I can do to improve the situation."
	Passivity	"Only my family member can make things better for me."
BEHAVIOUR	Failing to achieve goals	Failing because my goals were too high or vague
	Failing to benefit from efforts	Not receiving reinforcement from myself or others for efforts made
	Failing to try anything at all	Doing nothing myself. Waiting for others to make changes
	Worrying	Spending considerable time worrying

Increasing hope

Place a check next to the thought patterns you have that reduce your hopefulness:
- ☐ all-or-nothing thinking
- ☐ catastrophic thinking
- ☐ negative self-talk
- ☐ helplessness
- ☐ passivity.

Place a check next to the behaviours you demonstrate that reduce your hopefulness:
- ☐ failing to achieve goals
- ☐ failing to benefit from efforts
- ☐ failing to try anything at all
- ☐ worrying.

Place a check next to the thought patterns you use that increase your hopefulness:
- ☐ optimism
- ☐ self-mastery or self-efficacy
- ☐ self-encouragement
- ☐ creativity.

Place a check next to the behaviours you demonstrate that increase your hopefulness:
- ☐ achieving goals
- ☐ reinforcing myself
- ☐ positive experiences
- ☐ learning from others.

Select one thought pattern to decrease or increase during the week, in order to increase your hopefulness:

_____

_____

Select one behaviour to decrease or increase during the week, in order to increase your hopefulness:

_____

_____

Sayings related to hopefulness

If I constantly and continuously look for positive, it will soon capture me and overwhelm me with its presence.

—Joseph Araza

Roads are filled with gravel, little stones that may trip or bruise you, just like in life. There are setbacks that will trip you; fall but stand up, for abrasions will heal. Setbacks are part of life; it comes as a package. Grit your teeth and continue walking.

—Chua Hui Min

Keep moving. Keep putting one foot in front of the other. Inch by inch, you will get closer to success.

—Ronnie Nijmeh

Success is going from failure to failure without a loss of enthusiasm.

—Winston Churchill

Life is full of competition and to go forward you have to beat the tough challenges that are in your way.

—Mohammad Ahmed Yasin

With a positive attitude, thoughts are toward trying again. Therefore, failure does not exist.

—John Eaglespirit Campbell

Great things are not done by impulse, but by a series of small things brought together.

—author unknown

Some of us have great runways already built for us. If you have one, take off! But if you don't have one, realize it is your responsibility to grab a shovel and build one for yourself and for those who will follow after you.

—Amelia Earhart

Encouragement is oxygen to the soul. Good work can never be expected from a worker without encouragement. No one ever climbed spiritual heights without it. No one ever lived without it.

—George Matthew Adams

If you're trying to get something right, but you are not motivated to keep on trying, remember: The person who finally got it right, couldn't do it until the time that he finally did it. So keep on trying, who knows if the next time you try will be the one that you get it right?

—Viviane Cornachini

Your greatest challenge isn't someone else. It's the aching in your lungs and the burning in your legs and the voice inside you that yells "Can't!" But you don't listen. You push harder and hear the voice that whispers "Can." And you realize that the person you thought you were is no match for the one you really are.

—author unknown

Although the world is full of suffering, it is full also of the overcoming of it.

—Helen Keller

Source: Most of these quotations were posted on www.motivateus.com.

Next steps

OBJECTIVES

· to enable group members to share with one another what they have accomplished during their involvement with the group
· to reinforce and celebrate gains that group members have made
· to encourage group members to consider how they will sustain these gains and continue making positive changes in their lives
· to enable group members to process their group experiences and say goodbye to one another
· to acquire feedback from group members

HANDOUTS

18-1: Changes
18-2: Feedback Form
18-3: List of Resources

SESSION OUTLINE

· Opening and announcements (approx. 5 min.)
· Check-in and review of last week's home practice (approx. 30 min.)
· Teaching and discussion (approx. 60 min.)
· Assigning of next week's home practice (approx. 5 min.)
· Closing (approx. 5 min.)

Teaching and discussion

NEXT STEPS

▶ **Distribute or turn to Handout 18-1: Changes. Ask the group members to take five minutes to complete it.**

Ask the group members to share the changes they have observed in themselves. What do they attribute these changes to?

Ask the group members to share what changes they would still like to make. What might help them to achieve this goal?

Ask if they would give permission for the facilitators to photocopy or record their responses to help in evaluating the program.

Congratulate the participants for having attended the group sessions and for having made so many gains since they began. Remind them that change takes time and occurs in small steps (one day at a time). The ending of group does not signal the end of change for them.

You may wish to share some motivational quotes. You can find many motivational books or websites with relevant quotes. Below are a few examples from Motivateus.com.

> "If you want to get something done . . . start."
> —Victor Scrivani

> "You will be successful at any work you do if you have strong determination and an iron will."
> —author unknown

> "Even in defeat, I see victory as I am made wiser and will be victorious in my next battle."
> —author unknown

SHARING RESOURCES

Ask the group members to share any resources that they have found helpful, such as books, groups or websites.

▶ **Distribute or turn to Handout 18-3: List of Resources.**

Talk about and, when possible, show books or websites on the list.

▶ **Distribute a list of local services, if this was not already done in Module 4: Finding Support.**

Talk about options for other services (e.g., groups, counselling, workshops) that might be helpful.

SAYING GOODBYE TO ONE ANOTHER

You may ask the participants to exchange gifts, express their appreciation for one another or share things that have inspired or encouraged them.

Gift giving

Ask the group members to give gifts to one another, using the following script:

> Think about the person to your left [or right]. If you could give him or her two gifts—one that is tangible and concrete, something they can see or touch, and another gift that is intangible and abstract, like a feeling or a thought—what would those two gifts be?

NOTE: This could also be done as homework following the previous session to allow clients time to think about it.

Give group members a few moments to think about their gifts if they have not already done so.

Ask each participant to tell the adjacent person what his or her gifts would be, and why.

Expressing appreciation

Ask the group members to comment on what they have learned from, and/or appreciated about, one another.

Comment on strengths that you have noticed in each participant and/or ways that he or she has contributed to the group.

Sharing inspiration

Ask the group members to share something that has encouraged them, given them hope or inspired them, which might be inspiring to other group members. This may be, for example, a saying, picture, memory, story, spiritual verse or prayer.

EVALUATING GROUP SESSIONS

▶ **Distribute a feedback form and ask that the group members complete it anonymously and return it to you when they leave.**

Explain that their feedback will help to improve the services for future clients. You may choose to use Handout 18-2: Feedback Form, or to use this as a guide for creating your own form.

Changes

Since you began the group

How have your feelings changed?

_____

_____

_____

How have your thoughts changed?

_____

_____

_____

How has your behaviour changed?

_____

_____

_____

How has your relationship changed?

_____

_____

_____

Now, at the end of the group

What changes would you like to sustain?

_____

_____

What will help you do this?

_____

_____

What other change would you like to make?

_____

_____

What will help you make this change?

_____

_____

_____

Feedback form

We would like to get some feedback from you about your participation in this program.

How helpful were the teaching and discussions for you?

1	2	3	4	5
Not at all helpful	Somewhat helpful	Moderately helpful	Helpful	Very helpful

How helpful were the handouts for you?

1	2	3	4	5
Not at all helpful	Somewhat helpful	Moderately helpful	Helpful	Very helpful

How helpful were the homework exercises for you?

1	2	3	4	5
Not at all helpful	Somewhat helpful	Moderately helpful	Helpful	Very helpful

Sessions I attended:
- ☐ Starting out
- ☐ Understanding substance use problems and their effects on families
- ☐ Taking care of yourself
- ☐ Finding support
- ☐ Managing stress
- ☐ Using religious and spiritual resources
- ☐ Staying safe and managing crises
- ☐ Grieving and coping
- ☐ Managing emotions
- ☐ Communicating effectively with a person who has a substance use problem
- ☐ Problem solving
- ☐ Setting goals and making change happen
- ☐ Responding to a person who has a substance use problem
- ☐ Supporting the recovery of a person with a substance use problem
- ☐ Setting limits with a person who has a substance use problem
- ☐ Helping children affected by substance use in the family
- ☐ Finding hope
- ☐ Next Steps
- ☐ Other

What I found most valuable or helpful about this program:

_____

_____

_____

What session(s) I found most beneficial and why:

_____

_____

What session(s) I found least helpful and why:

_____

_____

What session I would like to have covered in greater depth:

_____

What session I would like to have done that was not included:

_____

Suggestion I have to improve this program:

_____

_____

_____

Thank you very much!

List of resources

BOOKS TO HELP FAMILIES AND PARTNERS AFFECTED BY SUBSTANCE USE

Beattie, M. (1986). *Codependent No More: How to Stop Controlling Others and Start Caring for Yourself.* Center City, MN: Hazelden.

Brown, S., Lewis, V. & Liotta, A. (2000). *The Family Recovery Guide: A Map for Healthy Growth.* Oakland, CA: New Harbinger Publications.

Meyers, J.M. & Wolf, B.L. (2004). *Get Your Loved One Sober: Alternatives to Nagging, Pleading, and Threatening.* Center City, MN: Hazelden.

Nakken, C. (2000). *Reclaim Your Family from Addiction: How Couples and Families Recover Love and Meaning.* Center City, MN: Hazelden.

Patterson-Sterling, C. (2004). *Rebuilding Relationships in Recovery: A Guide to Healing Relationships Impacted by Addiction.* Philadelphia, PA: Xlibris Corporation.

Shirley, K.J. (2000). *Resilient Marriage: From Alcoholism & Adversity to Relationship Growth.* Rowman and Littlefield.

Woititz, J. & Ackerman, R. (2002). *The Complete ACOA Sourcebook: Adult Children of Alcoholics at Home, at Work, and in Love.* Health Communications Inc.

BOOKS TO HELP COUPLES WANTING TO IMPROVE THEIR RELATIONSHIP

Cluris, D.M. (2004). *Lesbian Couples: A Guide to Creating Healthy Relationships.* Berkeley, CA: Seal Press.

Gottman, J. (1999). *The Seven Principles for Making Marriage Work.* New York: Three Rivers Press.

Gottman, J. (2002). *The Relationship Cure: A Five-Step Guide to Strengthening Your Marriage, Family and Friendships.* New York, Three Rivers Press.

Hendrix, H. (2005). *Getting the Love You Want.* New York: Pocket Books.

Leonhard, G. & Mast, J. (1997). *Feathering Your Nest: An Interactive Workbook and Guide to a Loving Lesbian Relationship.* Yarmouth, NS: Rising Tide Press.

Lerner, H. (1989). *The Dance of Intimacy: A Woman's Guide to Courageous Acts of Change in Key Relationships.* New York: Harper and Row.

Lerner, H. (1993). *The Dance of Deception: Truth-Telling in Women's Relationships.* New York: HarperCollins.

Lerner, H. (2001). *The Dance of Anger: A Woman's Guide to Changing the Patterns of Intimate Relationships.* New York: HarperCollins.

Lerner, H. (2001). *The Dance of Connection: How to Talk to Someone When You're Mad, Hurt, Scared, Frustrated, Insulted, Betrayed, or Desperate.* New York: HarperCollins.

BOOKS TO HELP PEOPLE COPE BETTER WITH LIFE

Davis, M., Robbins-Eshelman, E. & McKay, M. (1995). *The Relaxation and Stress Reduction Workbook* (5th ed.). Oakland, CA: New Harbinger Publications.

Greenerger, D. & Padesky, C. (1995). *Mind over Mood: Change How You Feel by Changing the Way You Think.* New York: Guilford Press.

Hollowell, E. (1997). *Worry: Hope and Help for a Common Condition.* New York: Ballantine Publishing Group.

James, J. & Friedman, R. (1998). *The Grief Recovery Handbook: The Action Program for Moving Beyond Death, Divorce and Other Losses* (rev. ed.). New York: HarperCollins.

Kabat-Zinn, J. (2005). *Full Catastrophe Living: Using the Wisdom of Your Body and Mind to Face Stress, Pain, and Illness.* New York: Bantam Dell.

Kushner, H. (2004). *When Bad Things Happen to Good People.* New York: Avon Books.

McKay, M. & Rogers, P. (2000). *The Anger Control Workbook.* Oakland, CA: New Harbinger Publications.

Prochaska, J., Norcross, J. & DiClemente, C. (1995). *Changing for Good: A Revolutionary Six-Stage Program for Overcoming Bad Habits and Moving Your Life Positively Forward.* New York: Avon Books.

Yapko, M. (1997). *Breaking the Patterns of Depression.* New York: Bantam Doubleday Dell.